Newts and Salamanders

Devin Edmonds

Newts and Salamanders

Project Team
Editor: Thomas Mazorlig
Indexer: Lucie Haskins
Cover Design: Mary Ann Kahn
Design: Patti Escabi

T.F.H. Publications
President/CEO: Glen S. Axelrod
Executive Vice President: Mark E. Johnson
Publisher: Christopher T. Reggio
Production Manager: Kathy Bontz

T.F.H. Publications, Inc.
One TFH Plaza
Third and Union Avenues
Neptune City, NJ 07753

Printed and bound in Indonesia
09 10 11 12 13   3 5 7 9 8 6 4 2

ISBN 978-0-7938-2899-9

Library of Congress Cataloging-in-Publication Data
Edmonds, Devin.
  Newts and salamanders : a complete guide to Caudata / Devin Edmonds.
      p. cm.
  Includes bibliographical references and index.
  ISBN 978-0-7938-2899-9 (alk. paper)
  1. Newts as pets. 2. Salamanders as pets. I. Title.
SF459.N48E36 2009
639.3'785—dc22
                          2008054756

This book has been published with the intent to provide accurate and authoritative information in regard to the subject matter within. While every reasonable precaution has been taken in preparation of this book, the author and publisher expressly disclaim responsibility for any error, omissions, or adverse effects arising from the use or application of the information contained herein. The techniques and suggestions are used at the reader's discretion and are not to be considered a substitute for veterinary care. If you suspect a medical problem consult your veterinarian.

The Leader In Responsible Animal Care For Over 50 Years!®
www.tfh.com

Table of Contents

Notophthalmus viridescens

Chapter 1

Salamanders and Newts as Pets

Those who are curious and persistent know the joy of rolling logs and netting ponds in search of newts and salamanders. It's fascinating to observe them in their natural habitat, yet the full range of interesting behavior they display is difficult to see outside of captivity. With a simple cage or aquarium setup, suitable environmental conditions, and a varied diet, most species live well. At the same time, advanced amphibian enthusiasts looking for a new project can find hundreds of salamanders and newts that provide the opportunity to keep and even breed a species few have before. Whether you are interested in an easily maintained but unique new pet or the chance to learn the ways of an uncommon amphibian, salamanders and newts deserve a serious look.

The red salamander (*Psuedotriton ruber*) is a colorful and fairly common salamander of the eastern United States.

Taxonomy

Taxonomy is the science of classifying things according to their perceived relationships. Today taxonomists classify living organisms into different groups by examining what they understand to be their evolutionary history. The most basic group is called a *species* (in some cases a species can be subdivided further into what are called subspecies; higher taxonomic groups as well can be subdivided). Species are placed within a *genus*, which usually contains other species that are closely related. Genera (plural for genus) are organized within *families*, which are sorted into different groups called *orders*, and these orders are then placed within different *classes* of organisms, which are then assigned to different *phyla*, which are then placed within the most inclusive groups of all, the *kingdoms* of animals, plants, etc.

All amphibians belong to the class Amphibia. Within this class, salamanders and newts are assigned to the order Caudata. Some authorities use Urodela instead as the name for this order. The relationships between members of the order Caudata are constantly under revision as new species are described and advances in molecular work allow biologists to sort out the evolutionary history of salamanders and newts. Currently there are ten families, containing more than 500 species.

Natural History of Salamanders and Newts

Of the slightly more than 6,000 described living amphibian species, only about 530 are tailed members of the order Caudata. This number continually changes as scientists describe new species and revise their taxonomy. Although there are far fewer species of salamanders and newts than frogs and toads, caudates rival their tailless counterparts in terms of diversity, inhabiting many different environments, where they have evolved fascinating adaptations.

Range and Habitat

Most salamanders and newts live in North America. Together, Mexico and the United States are home to nearly 300 species, containing representatives of nine of the ten families of Caudata. Only a couple of dozen salamanders inhabit South America. All but two are members of the intriguing genus *Bolitoglossa*, some of which are arboreal and live above ground in water-holding plants. There are just over 100 species of salamanders in Europe and Asia. Many of the common ones found for sale in the pet trade, like the Chinese fire-bellied newt (*Cynops orientalis*) and the fire salamander (*Salamandra salamandra*), are native to that part of the world. With the exception of four species found in the extreme north of the continent, salamanders and newts are absent from Africa.

Salamanders and newts are found around the world, so it's no surprise that they inhabit many different environments. Some salamanders are terrestrial, living on land in moist leaf

What's a Caudate?

Among amphibian hobbyists, the word "caudate" refers to any member of the order Caudata, meaning any salamander, newt, siren, mudpuppy, or other tailed amphibian not of the caecilian order Gymnophiona. The word "caudate" can also refer to anything that is tailed or has a tail-like appendage, but in this book it will be used as outlined above.

Salamander or Newt

There is no biological distinction between salamanders and newts. The word newt is typically used to describe a salamander that has some of the following characteristics:

- It is a member of the family Salamandridae.
- Its costal grooves (vertical grooves along the side of the body) are not clearly visible.
- It lives terrestrially while maturing after completing metamorphosis or is seasonally aquatic.
- Its skin texture is rougher than the typical salamander's.

litter or burrows, venturing into water only to breed. Other species are semi-aquatic and spend their time both in and out of water. Newts characteristically live a two-part life after completing metamorphosis, first living terrestrially and then returning to the water either seasonally or permanently once they reach sexual maturity. There are also many fully aquatic salamanders that never leave the water. These include the mudpuppies and the olm (family Proteidae), as well as the eel-like amphiumas (family Amphiumidae) and sirens (family Sirenidae). Many of these aquatic salamanders retain their larval gills as adults.

Physical Features

Among amphibians, the defining physical feature of newts and salamanders is their long tail. Four small legs protrude from the slender bodies of all except the sirens, which lack hind limbs. Like most other amphibians, salamanders have permeable smooth skin that is moistened by mucous glands. The skin serves not only as a boundary layer but also as a means of respiration. Over half of all salamanders breathe exclusively through their skin and lack lungs completely. In certain salamanders and newts, the skin is attractively patterned. These contrasting bright colors often serve as a warning to potential predators, making them aware of the salamander's or newt's poisonous nature.

In terms of size, most salamanders are small animals, though there are exceptions. The largest of all amphibians is the Chinese giant salamander (*Andrias davidianus*), which has been recorded as growing to over 5 feet (1.5 m) in length. These endangered monster amphibians inhabit cool mountain streams in China, rarely ever leaving the water. On the other end of the spectrum is the tiny salamander *Thorius arboreus*. Native to parts of Mexico, adults measure slightly over 0.6 inches (1.5 cm) in total length.

North America is home to more than half of all salamander species, including all of the eel-like amphiumas (*Amphiuma means* in this photo).

Feeding

Salamanders are predators, feeding on most any animal small enough to fit into their mouths. For those of average size, this means a diet of worms, snails, slugs, spiders, insects, and insect larvae. Large terrestrial species like the tiger salamander (*Ambystoma tigrinum*), can eat small mice and other vertebrates. Some aquatic salamanders consume fish in addition to aquatic invertebrates such as crustaceans and worms. Most salamanders and newts rely heavily on visual cues to locate a meal, homing in on prey using size, shape, and movement as visual signs of food. The odor of prey also plays an important role. Many salamanders and newts sniff food before consuming it to ensure it's palatable.

Reproduction

There are many ways in which salamanders and newts reproduce. Most breed near or in water so that the resulting aquatic larvae have a place to develop. Streams, rivers, ponds, vernal pools, and drainage ditches are all used as breeding sites, depending on species. Many salamanders and newts attach their eggs to aquatic plants, while others prefer submerged rocks or wood. Still others lay eggs next to water under logs or moss. As the eggs develop, some species guard them, not only defending their eggs against possible insect predators but also keeping them moist. It can take some salamander larvae years to metamorphose, though most take no more than half a year under normal conditions.

Amphibian Population Declines and Extinctions

Scientists have documented catastrophic amphibian population declines throughout the world. The World Conservation Union estimates that one third of all amphibians are threatened with extinction. Among the disappearing amphibians are numerous salamanders and newts. While their declines have not been researched as well as those of frogs and toads, it is clear that they are in trouble.

Habitat destruction is one of the largest threats facing salamanders and newts. As the human population grows, it uses more resources, often at a cost to the environment. Agricultural activity, logging, stream pollution, urbanization, and wetland drainage alter and destroy newt and salamander habitats. As our population increases it impinges on those of amphibians, but much can be done to change this. Protecting important breeding sites for newts and salamanders is vital, which entails the preservation of vernal pools and ponds used for reproduction. With many sala-

Many caudate species depend on vernal pools for breeding, including the spotted salamander.

Land-Loving Salamanders

A handful of salamanders breed on land rather than in water. Here the eggs undergo direct development, with metamorphosis occurring in the egg. After some time, miniature versions of the adult salamanders hatch out, having skipped the typical aquatic larval stage. Familiar species that breed in this way include redback salamanders (*Plethodon cinereus* and *P. serratus*), the arboreal salamander (*Aneides lugubris*), and ensatinas (*Ensatina eschscholtzii*).

manders living in or near forests, forest management is also important to their conservation.

Also threatening the existence of newts and salamanders is a recently described fungus called *Batrachochytrium dendrobatidis*. This fungus belongs to a class of fungi commonly referred to as chytrids. Once present in an environment, it can wipe out nearly all amphibians. It is unclear exactly how this fungus is spreading, but it has now been documented around the world, and as a result amphibians are disappearing even in seemingly pristine habitats.

Handling

Salamanders and newts should not be handled. The salts and oils naturally produced by human hands can irritate their sensitive skin. There is also a risk that handling causes harmful substances, such as lotion or soap residue, to come into contact with them. The benefit from lack of handling is not only to the salamander, though; it's also best for you and your health if you refrain from holding your pets. Most of the common newts and salamanders in the pet trade are poisonous. Unless you eat your pet salamander, you have little to worry about, but leave them alone to be on then safe side. When you must hold a salamander or newt—such as during transport or a cage cleaning—the best bet is to do so with moist hands or to use a small net. Thoroughly wash your hands before and after handling any amphibian.

Purchasing a Newt or Salamander

There are a number of ways to acquire newts and salamanders. Each has its advantages and disadvantages, and it's worth exploring all before getting your new amphibian.

Breeders

The hands-down best place to acquire a salamander or newt is from a breeder. It may seem strange that there are people who specialize in breeding caudates, but they do exist. In fact, you might be able to find one in your own town or city. You can locate breeders through local herpetological societies and on the Internet. Breeders provide healthy captive-bred caudates and also can give you reliable information about their care. Unfortunately, only a handful of species are bred consistently in captivity, so it may be difficult to find the certain species you wish to work with from a breeder.

Pet Stores

Pet stores regularly stock a few common newts and occasionally a salamander or two. At the store you can inspect both the individual animal and its captive environment prior to making a purchase. Few pet stores are particularly knowledgeable when it comes to the care of amphibians, and it's not uncommon for newts and salamanders to be housed in crowded con-

The Ten Families of Caudata

Family	
Ambystomatidae	Mole Salamanders: The members of Ambystomatidae are called mole salamanders because most of the 32 species spend considerable time underground in burrows.
Amphiumidae	Amphiumas/Congo Eels: Long, slender, and aquatic; all three species within Amphiumidae are native to the southeast United States.
Cryptobranchidae	Giant Salamanders: The three species in Cryptobranchidae truly are giants, growing to incredible sizes and living many years in cool streams.
Dicamptodontidae	Pacific Giant Salamanders: The four species in Dicamptodontidae closely resemble mole salamanders morphologically, but they differ genetically.
Hynobiidae	Asiatic Salamanders: All but one of the 50 or so species live in Asia. They are closely related to the giant salamanders and similarly fertilize eggs externally.
Plethodontidae	Lungless Salamanders: Containing more than 350 species, Plethodontidae is a diverse salamander family. Their nasolabial groove (a slit near their mouth) and lack of lungs differentiate them from other caudates.
Proteidae	Mudpuppies, Waterdogs, and Olms: All members of Proteidae are fully aquatic and retain external gills as adults. The European native olm (*Proteus anguinus*) is the only species found outside of North America.
Rhyacotritonidae	Torrent Salamanders: Native to the northwest United States, there are four species in this family. They live in coniferous forests and breed in streams.
Salamandridae	True Salamanders: Salamandridae contains many of the common species kept in captivity, including the popular fire salamander and fire-bellied newt.
Sirenidae	Sirens: The four sirens are the only salamanders that lack hind limbs. They are fully aquatic and retain their bushy external gills as adults.

Captive-Bred Caudates

A handful of newts and salamanders are bred in captivity regularly. These captive-bred amphibians are your best option if you're a first-time salamander keeper. Species regularly bred in captivity include crested and marbled newts (*Triturus* spp.), alpine newts (*Mesotriton alpestris*), axolotls (*Ambystoma mexicanum*), Spanish ribbed newts (*Pleurodeles waltl*), and fire salamanders (*Salamandra salamandra*).

ditions. For this reason, choose the stores you go to wisely, paying close attention to how they keep their amphibians.

Herp Dealers

Reptile and amphibian dealers supply both pet stores and individuals. They can be located on the Internet and usually have significantly lower prices than pet stores. These cheap prices may come with an added cost in the quality of animals. Additionally, the shipping and handling fees often outweigh the low prices, making dealers considerably more expensive than other sources if you're purchasing only a small group of salamanders. One way to overcome this is to order with some other herp keepers and share the cost of the shipping.

Herp Shows

At herp shows, reptile and amphibian dealers, breeders, and sometimes specialty pet stores meet in one place to show and sell their animals. They are an excellent source for acquiring new pets because the animals can be inspected before they're purchased and prices are generally low. Unfortunately, newts and salamanders are underrepresented at these events, and sometimes aren't even present. You can find a local herp show by searching the Internet or paging through the back of reptile/amphibian (and sometimes also aquarium) magazine

Collecting

If you live within the range of the species you wish to work with, and it is not bred in captivity, consider spending a night outside with a headlamp in search of a salamander to keep. Collecting your own salamander or newt is an excellent way to acquire one of the many species that aren't produced in captivity, because you don't fuel the mass commercial collection of salamanders that supplies the pet trade. An even better option is to collect larvae or a few eggs to raise. Never release a salamander collected from the wild back to its natural habitat, because even an apparently healthy amphibian can introduce pathogens foreign to your local populations once kept in captivity. Instead, capture a salamander only if you intend to keep it for the remainder of its life. Also, before going out to capture a newt or salamander, check with local laws to ensure that such capture is legal—including making sure the species you desire is not threatened or endangered. In many areas a permit is required to collect amphibians.

Selecting a Salamander or Newt

Once you find a suitable source for the species you want to keep and have thoroughly researched its care, the next step is to select a healthy one. First, look at how they are being housed. Note the temperature they are being kept at, because those housed in inappropriately warm conditions sometimes succumb to health problems several weeks down the line. Also inspect the cage setup itself, paying close attention to whether it's appropriate for the species being housed in it. Salamanders or newts housed the wrong way at the vendor's may develop problems once in your care.

If you decide to collect your own sala-manders, obey the relevant local laws and only collect more abundant species, such as the red eft in many areas.

Healthy salamanders typically remain hidden during the day unless disturbed, so avoid individuals that actively are roaming about their enclosure. Newts and aquatic species may be more visible than secretive terrestrial salamanders. Avoid all types that show symptoms of health probles such as clouded eyes, irregularly colored skin, missing digits or parts of the tail, or unusual behavior.

Bringing Your Salamander Home

Salamanders and newts can be transported a number of ways. The easiest is to place them into a small sturdy plastic container such as a deli cup. A couple of ventilation holes can be punched through the sides if the animal(s) will be in it for an extended period of time. Inside the container, place a small piece of moist paper towel for terrestrial or semi-aquatic species. Fully aquatic salamanders should be provided with very shallow water. Plastic bags can be used instead of plastic containers, but take care that they are sealed with plenty of air inside. The container or bag can then be placed into a small cooler so that the temperature doesn't fluctuate. On warm days, make sure to allow your car to cool before bringing your new newt or salamander home.

Ambystoma mexicanum

Chapter 2

Housing

The most important part of keeping newts and salamanders in captivity is the environment they're housed in. Setups can be simple and hygienically bare or more complex, incorporating live plants to create detailed miniature landscapes. Often the best habitat for your newt or salamander lies somewhere between the two, and over time you can develop your own way to house your pet salamander, which is an enjoyable part of their care.

Salamanders and newts inhabit many different environments, and different species require different types of housing. You can sort most salamanders and newts into one of three categories: fully aquatic, semi-aquatic, or terrestrial. Fully aquatic species need to be kept in aquaria, with the maintenance of their habitat being similar to that of an aquarium for fish. Semi-aquatic species require different cage setups, with a portion of land emerging from the water to allow easy access out. The size of this land area depends on the species of newt or salamander being kept. For terrestrial species, only a small water dish is required, with the rest of the cage containing a suitable soil or other substrate and a few hide spots.

The size of the enclosure used to house a salamander or newt depends on the species being kept. Small salamanders, such as two-lined salamanders (*Eurycea* spp.) or a red eft (*Notophthalmus viridescens*), may require no more room than a standard 5.5 gallon (21-liter) aquarium. Aggressive, active, or large species, like warty newts (*Paramesotriton* spp.), mudpuppies (*Necturus maculosus*), and the two-toed amphiuma (*Amphiuma means*) do best in large enclosures. An alternative to using a traditional glass aquarium can be found at the local home supply or hardware store. Plastic storage containers are excellent newt and salamander homes because they are lightweight and affordable. The tops can be fitted with fiberglass window screen for ventilation.

When kept in groups, salamanders and newts can display fascinating behavior. To accommodate this, it's important that adequate space be provided. Males in particular can be quite aggressive towards one another. In the wild, they often occupy distinct territories. If you choose to keep multiple individuals together, ensure that there is space for all, especially if working with a species known to be aggressive. It may be advantageous to house certain species either individually or in male/female pairs.

Many salamanders, including the commonly available axolotl, are completely aquatic animals.

The live plants in this crocodile newt's tank help maintain good water quality.

Housing Aquatic Newts and Salamanders

Fully aquatic salamanders, such as paddle-tailed newts (*Pachytriton* spp.), the axolotl (*Ambystoma mexicanum*), sirens (Sirenidae), and amphiumas (Amphiumidae), need to be housed in aquariums. The larvae of salamanders and newts also require aquatic habitats. There are essentially two approaches to housing these aquatic amphibians. One method relies heavily on bacteria that naturally grow in aquariums to control waste that accumulates. The other involves a more sterile setup, using a bare-bottom tank and a siphon to regularly remove waste. Both styles of housing work well, though larger caudates are best housed in simple setups because of the larger amount of waste they excrete. No matter the type of setup, use the largest size aquarium possible to house aquatic and semi-aquatic salamanders, because the greater the volume of water, the more stable the water quality will be.

Water Quality

Maintaining good water quality is essential to keeping your aquatic newts or salamanders healthy. Most common problems encountered with aquatic amphibians can be attributed to poor water quality, so it's important to understand how to keep the water safe for your pets. The interconnected chemical and biological processes that naturally take place within aquariums may seem overwhelming, but understanding the basics is important to amphibian care.

Aquarium test kits are available at pet stores and allow you to monitor various conditions within your salamander's enclosure. Most important is monitoring the ammonia, nitrite, and nitrate. Ammonia and nitrite should not be present in a healthy aquarium, and the nitrate should remain under 20 ppm (parts per million). Additionally, you may find it helpful to test the hardness and pH of your water, though only in extreme situations are these conditions outside of a safe range. If you don't want to purchase your own test kits, many pet shops and tropical fish specialty pet stores will test the water for you if you bring them a water sample.

Water straight from the tap can be saturated with dissolved gases. This is problematic for captive amphibians, so if you use tap water, allow it to sit in an uncovered container for a day or two to let gases dissipate.

Nitrification Beneficial bacteria are largely in charge of maintaining water quality in an aquarium. These microscopic unicellular organisms feed on waste in the tank. Of particular importance are nitrifying bacteria. Ammonia (NH_3)—toxic to newts, salamanders, and most other aquatic animals—is formed naturally in all aquariums as waste decomposes. One type of nitrifying bacteria feed on the dangerous ammonia as it's produced and turn it into nitrite (NO_2^-), which is then turned into the less harmful nitrate (NO_3^-) by other bacteria. Nitrate is what you are responsible for removing from the aquarium with partial water changes. Additionally, live plants help keep nitrate levels in line. Keep the nitrifying bacteria in an aquarium healthy and chances are good that your aquatic animals will also remain in good health.

Bacteria grow on nearly every surface in an aquarium, so it's advantageous to create as much surface area as possible to support large colonies of these helpful microorganisms. You can use rocks or artificial aquarium decorations with rough surfaces to achieve this, as well as filter media designed to provide large surface areas for bacteria to grow on. Gravel is also a great way to provide growing space for helpful bacteria. To keep your bacteria colonies healthy, the surfaces on which they grow should not be cleaned all at once. Never take all of the gravel out of an aquarium and clean it thoroughly. Instead, use an aquarium vacuum to siphon through the gravel every few weeks. It's also good practice to clean rocks, driftwood, and other aquarium furnishings alternately rather than all at once so that bacteria colonies established on these items are given time to grow back between cleanings.

Water Hardness and pH Two chemical aspects of water quality that concern many people are the hardness of their water and its pH. Water hardness involves the water's mineral content, in particular the calcium and magnesium ions in the water. In all but the most extreme conditions, as long as the hardness of the water is stable and does not vary, you do not have to worry about it. In fact, playing around with chemical additives to adjust the hardness can do more harm than good, creating unhealthy fluctuating conditions that are stressful for aquatic animals.

The pH of water is a measure of the acidity or alkalinity (basicity). The pH scale ranges from 0 to14, with 7 being neutral. Readings below 7 indicate acidic conditions, and above 7 designate basic or alkaline conditions. As with water hardness, pH is not the most important component of water quality provided it's stable. Most aquatic amphibians do well in water with a near-neutral pH. Avoid acidic conditions where the pH is below 6.0, as well as those above 8.5 (note that these guidelines are somewhat species-dependent). Rather than add aquarium chemical additives to increase or decrease the pH, it's a safer strategy to simply place a bag of crushed limestone (to counteract low pH) or peat moss (to help counteract high pH) into the filter, which will gradually and safely change the pH over time, though this is rarely required.

Chlorine and Chloramines A number of chemicals are added to our drinking water, some of which are unsafe for amphibians. Chlorine and chloramines are of particular concern. Over time, these chemicals harm newts and salamanders and can even kill them. To rid your water of chlorine and chloramines, use an aquarium water conditioner.

An alternative method is to use water that has been filtered through a reverse-osmosis (RO) membrane. Water processed by reverse osmosis can be purchased at grocery stores or some specialty pet shops. It is free of high concentrations of chlorine, chloramines, and

Cycling

Nitrifying bacteria take time to grow. They will not develop without a source of ammonia. "Cycling an aquarium" means developing these helpful bacteria, a process that can take anywhere from three to six weeks. For this reason, it's best to set up the habitat for your aquatic newts or salamanders well in advance of getting them.

To cycle an aquarium, ammonia needs to be introduced. There are many methods for doing this. Fish excrete ammonia as waste, so by placing a few hardy species, such as white cloud minnows (*Tanichthys albonubes*) or guppies (*Poecilia reticulata*), into your aquarium you can effectively cycle it. These fish should be removed once amphibians are introduced. Placing frozen fish food or a piece of cocktail shrimp into the water is another good strategy for cycling a tank. As the food decays, ammonia forms and nitrifying bacteria grow. Remove fish food or shrimp once ammonia is detected.

Whichever method you choose, it's important to test the water frequently for ammonia and nitrite. Following an initial ammonia spike, nitrite will start to form and the ammonia will decrease. Several weeks later, the nitrite should spike, then decrease, and nitrate will develop. Once nitrate is present and both nitrite and ammonia read zero, do a water change to bring the nitrate to a safe level. At this point your tank is fully cycled and you can add your newts or salamanders.

other impurities. If you keep many aquatic animals, you might consider purchasing an RO filtration unit yourself. Add aquarium products that contain salts, minerals, and other dissolvable solids to this pure water to create the conditions favorable for amphibians.

Filtration

An important part of maintaining proper water quality is filtration. There are many types of filters, and it can be confusing trying to navigate your way through the dozens of styles and brands available at most pet stores. When large volumes of water are used and live plants are grown, a filter often isn't needed as long as frequent partial water changes are performed. For most setups, though, the right filter is the key to successful aquarium maintenance, allowing you to easily remove captured waste and toxins.

Filters operate by moving aquarium water through some sort of medium. There are essentially three types of filtration that filters provide: mechanical, chemical, and biological. The mechanical aspect of filtration involves some sort of fabric or foam through which water circulates to catch suspended particles. Chemical filtration consists of media, such as activated carbon and ammonia remover, that chemically change the water quality. The third object of a filter, the biological filtration, operates by providing a medium that has a large amount of surface area on which beneficial bacteria grow.

Most newts, such as southern crested newts (*Triturus karelinii*), do not tolerate poor water quality, so using a filter is recommended.

Sponge Filters

An oldie but goodie, sponge filters have been used for decades because they are practical and effective. They consist of a vertical tube and a foam sponge that sit inside the aquarium. Water is drawn through the sponge, where both mechanical and biological filtration occurs. Sponge filters are ideal for the majority of aquatic newts and salamanders and are the best way to filter small aquariums that are stocked lightly. They also are perfect for filtering the water of salamander or newt larvae. Maintenance involves rinsing the foam sponge every couple weeks.

Submersible Power Filters

Submersible power filters are good for

filtering moderately sized aquariums and for creating small currents for tank inhabitants that prefer moving water. They sit inside the aquarium, submerged under water. Many submersible power filters have an adjustable flow rate, which for most aquatic newts and salamanders should remain on the lowest setting. A rock or piece of driftwood can also be used to deflect the output.

Power Filters Power filters are ideal for many aquatic setups. They hang over the back of the aquarium. In the newer styles of these filters, a pump draws water in through an intake tube that sits inside the tank, and the water flows back into the tank after passing through a filter. Filter media usually consist of an easily replaced bag; the bag may or may not be equipped with activated charcoal. As water flows through this bag, suspended particles are captured on its walls, while the activated charcoal inside helps remove dissolved organic wastes, odors, and discoloration from the water chemically. Plan to replace this bag monthly. Hang-on-the-tank power filters are best for filtering medium to large aquariums that house fairly messy inhabitants.

Undergravel Filters Undergravel filters are undesirable for filtering aquatic newt and salamander tanks. These filters operate by creating a partial vacuum under the raised bottom plate of the filter, thereby drawing water (and waste) down into the gravel, relying on the bacteria that live throughout the gravel's surfaces to maintain water quality. In my opinion, they are best passed over for better options because over time it is common for excess wastes to accumulate beneath filter plates, causing water quality problems.

Canister Filters The big boys of the filtration world are the canister filters. They provide a large area for filtration media within a canister that usually sits underneath the aquarium.

Amphibian Escapes

Many aquatic caudates are excellent escape artists, squeezing their way through the tiniest of gaps. The intake tube of a power or canister filter provides just the right amount of space for many to fit through, so wedge foam plugs in any opening created by these devices. It can be helpful to keep the water depth in an aquarium several inches below the top to prevent your aquatic amphibians from escaping.

You will need to perform regular water changes even when using a filter and lots of live plants, as in this fire-bellied newt enclosure.

Input and output tubes run up and into the aquarium from below. Canister filters work exceptionally well for filtering large volumes of water but are overkill for small aquariums.

Water Changes

In order to maintain a healthy aquarium or semi-aquatic environment, some of the water must be replaced periodically. In a well-planted established aquarium, 15 to 30 percent of the water should be replaced every two weeks. In more sterile setups, partial water changes are best performed once or twice a week. You can use a section of hose or tubing to siphon detritus off the bottom of the tank in aquariums without substrate. Never change all of the water in an aquarium. Doing so stresses the inhabitants and removes many of the helpful bacteria that are in charge of controlling water quality.

The water you use to fill the tank back up with after some is removed is an important consideration. To avoid potentially deadly temperature shocks, make sure the water going back into the tank is the same temperature as the water already in it. It's best to let replacement water sit in an open container for a day or two before doing a water change. This allows tap water, which can be oversaturated with dissolved gases, to settle and become safe for your amphibians. Treat water with a conditioner to remove chlorine, chloramines, and heavy metals it might contain during this time.

The Natural Aquarium

A traditional aquarium with a filter, layer of gravel, and

live plants can be used to house many caudates. These systems, once established, are a superb method for displaying small aquatic species. The beneficial bacteria that grow within these tanks help maintain water quality in conjunction with live plants. These aquariums require minimal maintenance, with partial (15 to 30 percent) water changes needing to be performed every other week and cleaning of the filter done once a month. It's best to set up the aquarium one to two months in advance of adding amphibians to it. During this time, nitrifying bacteria develop. (See the sidebar in this chapter about cycling an aquarium for more information.)

The gravel used in the aquarium is an important consideration. It serves both as a surface on which helpful bacteria grow and as a medium to grow live plants in. Additionally, it must be safe for newts and salamanders. Small pea gravel is preferable because plants can root easily in it and it provides a large amount of surface area on which helpful bacteria grow. Unfortunately, small-grade gravel can fit into the mouths of aquatic amphibians, and if swallowed, sometimes causes problems. To prevent this, place a layer of large gravel that your newts or salamanders can not swallow over an initial layer of small pea gravel. Use several inches (7.6 cm) of gravel to form a thick layer on the bottom. Alternatively, a thin layer of fine aquarium sand can be used as a substrate; though it will likely be accidentally ingested by your aquatic pets, it usually passes without problems.

If you use gravel as a substrate, be sure the individual pieces are too big for your newts to swallow, as shown here with an eastern newt.

Annoying Algae

Though visually unpleasant, the brown and green film, hair, and slime that coats aquarium glass and décor is not necessarily bad. They're all different types of algae, which inevitably grow in all healthy aquariums. Keep lighting to a minimum (10-12 hours a day) and perform frequent partial water changes to slow down algal growth. You can use a razor blade and algae pad to effectively remove it from an aquarium. If it grows back quickly or seems to take over the tank, consider testing your water for nitrates, phosphates, and silicates, all of which contribute to algae problems. Growing aquatic plants can also help counter algae.

Driftwood, rocks, terracotta flower pots, and aquarium decorations can serve as hide spots for aquatic newts and salamanders in natural aquarium setups. Ensure that all heavy aquarium decorations are placed flat against the bottom of the tank rather than on top of gravel so that they do not shift over time. Avoid using rocks such as marble, limestone, and anything with a metallic shine, because these may negatively affect water quality. Instead, good choices include slate, granite, and quartz. If you are unsure whether a rock is safe to put into an aquarium, try placing a few drops of vinegar on it. If the vinegar sizzles, the rock is unsafe.

Live plants are an important part of an aquarium. Though they are not required, it's advantageous to grow live plants because they use the nitrates produced by nitrifying bacteria and provide cover for aquatic amphibians. Unfortunately, not every plant grows well in the cool waters most aquatic salamanders prefer. Good species to choose include anacharis (*Elodea densa*), coldwater pennyworts (*Hydrocotyle* spp.), guppy grass (*Najas guadalupensis*), and vallisnerias (*Vallisneria* spp.) Floating vegetation such as Amazon frogbit (*Limnobium laevigatum*) and floating watermoss (*Salvinia natans*) are also useful. Ensure that live plants are planted appropriately. While most species should be planted directly into gravel, others like anubias (*Anubias* spp.) and java fern (*Microsorum pteropus*) do well only when their bottoms are not smothered by a dense substrate; they should be tied with thin monofilament fishing line to a piece of wood or rock, Some plant species should be left to float.

Lighting is very important for growing live plants. In shallow aquariums, two standard fluorescent tubes running the length of the tank do the job. In deeper tanks, you may find compact fluorescent lighting to be best. Because aquatic newts and salamanders are most comfortable in dim conditions, provide dark caves and hide spots. Floating plants also help filter out light and provide a sense of security for your amphibians.

A Plague of Snails

Snails are introduced into aquariums accidentally, usually hitching a ride in as eggs on live plants. They can quickly multiply, taking over a tank in just a few months. Though snails are not harmful, if you wish to get rid of these tiny shelled creatures do not use commercially available "snailicides," because they are dangerous to amphibians. Instead, manually remove snails. A good strategy is to place a couple of slices of zucchini in the aquarium overnight. Snails flock to these slices in great numbers and can be removed en masse by pulling the sliced vegetable out the following morning.

The Simple Aquarium

In contrast to natural planted aquariums are simple practical designs. The latter are perfect for messy large caudates, which have a tendency to disrupt the aesthetics of a planted tank. Simple designs also work well for raising large numbers of larvae and young aquatic salamanders. Without a lot of clutter, the inhabitants within a simple setup can be monitored easily, and for this reason they are often the best way to initially house aquatic species to ensure they're in good health.

A bare bottom with no substrate is what sets a simple setup apart from a more natural approach. Bare-bottom aquariums are safer because there is no gravel or substrate for a salamander to accidentally ingest, and they make maintenance a cinch, allowing you to siphon excess waste out of the aquarium. This will need to be done frequently, in some situations daily. But without a thick layer of gravel, the beneficial bacteria that help with the water quality have less surface area to grow on. To make up for this, choose a filter that provides plenty of biological filtration. Sponge filters are perfect if you're housing only a couple of small salamanders or larvae, but most often the best choice is a power filter that incorporates some sort of porous medium or media to support bacteria.

You can use aquarium decorations, driftwood, flower pots, and PVC pipe segments for hiding spots so your salamanders or newts feel secure in these barren setups. Make certain that cage furnishings do not move around when placed on the glass bottom of the tank. Floating vegetation can also be grown on the water's surface to filter out light and help maintain good water quality.

Housing Semi-Aquatic Newts and Salamanders

Many newts and salamanders are considered semi-aquatic, meaning they spend time both in and out of the water. Commonly kept semi-aquatic species include the Chinese fire-bellied newt (*Cynops orientalis*), alpine newt (*Mesotriton alpestris*), and rough-skinned newt (*Taricha granulosa*). It's important to consider the specific species for which a semi-aquatic setup is intended. Some species are more aquatic than others, requiring only a small floating landmass onto which to occasionally emerge. Others prefer a greater range of conditions, favoring a large land area of a size equal to the water portion of their tank. Some semi-aquatic newts go through terrestrial and aquatic stages, changing over the course of their

Slipping Salamanders

Sometimes aquatic salamanders lose their footing on bare-bottomed enclosures, sliding around as if they were walking on ice. Scattering a few easily removed flat rocks around the bottom can give your amphibian companions some appreciated footing.

Semi-aquatic enclosure suitable for housing dusky salamanders.

life, and for these species it can be best to switch from a terrestrial setup to an aquatic one over time rather than attempt to create both simultaneously.

The most basic semi-aquatic setup consists of a simple aquarium design (outlined above) with a lowered water level and some sort of object emerging from the water's surface. The object can be a pile of securely stacked rocks, a large piece of driftwood, a cork bark float, or a plastic container filled with gravel and soil. Both emergent and floating vegetation are useful ways of creating objects for small semi-aquatic newts to rest on. The water portion of the tank can be treated and maintained as an aquarium, with partial water changes being performed regularly and a small sponge filter being used to capture small suspended particles in the water column. Some semi-aquatic species prefer fast-flowing, well-aerated water, and in this case a submersible power filter can be used instead of a sponge filter.

An alternative to stacking objects in water to create a land area is to use a glass divider. Glass cut to fit the width of an aquarium can be secured in place using silicone sealant. Avoid using clear acrylic or Plexiglas in place of glass as your divider, because those plastics do not adhere as well to glass aquariums and may warp over time. Also steer clear of sealant that contains mold inhibitors, instead opting for brands labeled as "aquarium-safe." Once the sealant is dry and tested for leaks, you can fill the land area with gravel to a depth of several inches, over which you can place fiberglass window screen, followed by an amphibian-safe soil mixture. Dried leaves and small piles of moss can cover the soil, and live plants, if desired, can be grown in the land area for added aesthetics and shelter. Use gently sloping secure rock piles and driftwood to allow easy access for your salamanders and newts to and from the water.

An elevated land area can also be created using gravel that is sloped to one end of an aquarium. In this case, the divider won't be waterproof, but if you keep the water level below the surface of the raised gravel, the land area will remain dry. Use rocks or heavy driftwood to help support the gravel. Over the land you can place a layer of large river rocks, sphagnum moss, and/or leaf mulch. This will prevent your pets from swallowing gravel. As time passes, the mound of gravel forming the land area will shift, and you may

Naturalistic semi-aquatic enclosure suitable for a number of different caudate species. The plant is a pothos, a hardy choice for terraria.

find it necessary to re-sculpt the slope several times a year.

Live plants are particularly advantageous in semi-aquatic setups. Species that grow both in and out of water can form trailing bridges between the two sections. Heartleaf philodendron (*Philodendron scandens*), pothos (*Scindapsus aureus*), and wandering Jew (*Tradescanta fluminensis*) are three readily available plants that can serve this purpose. Additionally, emergent plants, able to grow with their leaves extending out of the water, can form terrestrial resting spots for smaller newts. Anubias (*Anubias* spp.) are good for this purpose, but they grow slowly, particularly in the cool water most newts and salamanders require. Parrot's feather (*Myriophyllum aquaticum*) is another good supportive emergent species to use.

Housing Terrestrial Newts and Salamanders

Easier to house than both aquatic and semi-aquatic caudates are those that spend their time on land. Species well suited to a terrestrial environment include tiger salamanders (*Ambystoma mavortium* and *A. tigrinum*) and other ambystomids, red efts, fire salamanders, and many lungless salamanders (family Plethodontidae). Salamanders and newts that require terrestrial setups are often secretive, many digging or burrowing their way out of view of humans.

Substrates

Where water quality is crucial to the captive care of aquatic amphibians, the substrate is what's most important for terrestrial ones. It's the medium on which they spend their days, and choosing the right substrate is important to their health. A good substrate holds moisture, permits proper osmoregulation, and is safe if accidentally ingested. There are many opinions about what is best, and you may find it useful to try a few different substrates over time.

Paper Towels The easiest and most practical substrate for terrestrial salamanders is paper towels. A moist sheet or two can be placed on the bottom of the enclosure, followed by wetted, crumpled pieces scattered around the cage to form hide spots. By piling several layers of these papers in one end, a moisture gradient can be provided, with those on the bottom being wetter than the towels exposed near the top. Paper towels should be replaced once a week, though in heavily stocked small enclosures daily cleaning may be necessary.

Mulches and Fir Bark Mulches can be used as substrates, but use caution when choosing one. Avoid those made from pine or cedar, because the oils in them are unsafe for amphibians. Fir bark or orchid bark can be used, but both have potential to cause impactions if accidentally ingested. They work best when blended into a soil mixture rather than used alone. Finely milled cypress mulch is a fairly good option. Unfortunately, it's most often made by feeding young cypress trees into wood chippers, aiding in the destruction of the wetlands that are important ecosystems for wild amphibians.

Many terrestrial salamanders—juvenile tiger salamander in this photo—will do well on a substrate of damp paper towels.

Coconut Husk Fiber Made from the ground-up hair-like fibers around coconut shells, coconut husk fiber makes an excellent substrate. It is moisture retentive and fairly safe if accidentally ingested by a salamander. Many pet stores sell it in dried compact bricks. When placed in warm water, it expands into a loose soil-like substance. Coconut husk fiber can be used alone or, even better, mixed with other ingredients to form the ideal substrate blend. Leaf compost, cypress mulch, shredded moss, and top soil can all be used for this purpose.

Top Soil The suitability of top soil as a substrate depends on where it was collected and how it has been treated. Without any additives, most top soil is a great option for terrestrial caudates. Read the words on the bag carefully, though. Top soil that contains manure, small stones, large amounts of clay, perlite, vermiculite, or added fertilizers should be avoided. As with coconut husk fiber, you may find it helpful to mix in other ingredients to the soil in order to give it the right consistency, or combine it in a 50/50 mix with coconut husk fiber.

Unsafe Substrates A handful of commonly used amphibian substrates are unsafe for terrestrial salamanders. Gravel should be avoided because it does not retain moisture and can be dangerous if accidentally swallowed. Large river rocks can be used in semi-aquatic setups but are best passed up for terrestrial ones. Peat moss and sphagnum moss are too acidic for use with most commonly available species and can potentially cause ion exchange problems for salamanders kept on either for extended periods of time. Green reptile moss sold at pet stores also is not an ideal substrate when used alone, but it can be mixed into soil with good results. Avoid reptile carpeting because it's abrasive and doesn't hold moisture well.

Deep Dirt

Burrowing salamanders love to dig, completely concealing themselves beneath a blanket of dirt. Unfortunately, this is not a great quality for a pet, at least partly because it makes it difficult to monitor them. Instead of using a deep layer of substrate, you might find it best to use only around an inch (2.5 cm). Over this, place plenty of cover in the form of corkbark, driftwood, and other hiding spots. These can easily be removed if you wish to view your slimy pet.

Cage Furnishings

Furnish the enclosure with suitable hide spots. Loose leaf litter can be used for smaller species to curl up in and burrow beneath. Collect this from a safe location, where pesticides and fertilizers are not used. If you want to sterilize it, you can put it in the microwave, though freshly collected leaf litter often contains an assortment of tiny invertebrates for small salamanders to feed on. Cork bark flats are ideal hiding spots, and when piled on top of each other form dry caves many terrestrial caudates enjoy taking shelter in. Driftwood, artificial plants, and commercially available reptile and amphibian hide spots are also good options. In housing for small terrestrial species, live plants such as pothos (*Scindapsus aureus*)

Moisture Gradients

Providing a moisture gradient within the substrate is important. This means that one end of the cage should stay slightly drier than the other, allowing your terrestrial salamander to regulate its bodily conditions. A good way to accomplish this is to raise one end of the cage an inch (2.5 cm) above the other. As a result, the higher end remains drier than the lower end. Another option is to stack pieces of bark or driftwood in one end of the cage, forming drier hide spots in between the wood.

and small ferns can be grown if lighting is provided. Larger terrestrial salamanders may uproot live plants.

Water Sources

Terrestrial salamanders and newts do not drink water. Instead, they absorb it through their skin. Provide an easily accessible dish of clean water for your salamanders to soak in. If chlorinated water is used, treat it with an appropriate aquarium tap water conditioner to remove chlorine, chloramines, and heavy metals. Change this water dish as needed. For species that soak often, this might mean daily water changes. For others, you may only need to replace the water a couple times a week. Though the stereotypical image of an amphibian is an animal that does equally well both in water and on land, many salamanders do not meet this notion and can drown in deep water. To avoid drowning, use a shallow water dish that is easy for your caudate to climb in and out of. Ceramic bowls, shallow plastic deli cups, and flower pot drainage trays are all good options.

Some salamanders rarely encounter standing water in the wild, and when a water dish is provided in captivity it is usually avoided. For these amphibians, you will not need to offer a water dish. Instead, maintain a moisture gradient throughout the substrate so that they can stay hydrated by moving about their enclosure. Many terrestrial plethodontids can be kept in this manner.

Cleaning and Maintenance

Whichever substrate you choose, you will need to replace it periodically. Paper towels need to be changed weekly at a minimum, sometimes as often as daily. If you use soil, mulch, or other organic substrate, expect to replace some or all of it several times a year. Exactly how often you need to do this will depend on how many salamanders you are keeping and how large the enclosure is. Densely stocked smaller tanks need their substrate replaced more often than large enclosures housing a single newt or salamander. A good way to tell whether the substrate needs to be replaced is the smell. A healthy environment for your newt or salamander should smell fresh—like a pile of leaves or the forest floor—and not sour or swampy.

Avoid using soaps or other chemicals for cleaning, because the residue left behind after their use could be unsafe. Instead, rely on hot tap water and a soap-free sponge for cleaning. A sharp razor blade is also a good cleaning tool. You can use it for scraping water spots and film off glass. To disinfect an enclosure, use a 10 percent bleach solution. Rinse the enclosure with hot water until the smell of bleach is gone, then allow it to air dry for the following day. A safer alternative to bleach is chlrohexidine, which is available from farm and veterinary supply companies. Iodine-based cleaners should be passed up for better options, because plastics can retain these chemicals.

Temperature Regulation

Salamanders and newts are ectotherms, meaning their body temperature depends on that of their surroundings. When kept outside of an appropriate temperature range, they decline in health quickly.

In general, newts and salamanders require cool conditions. The exact temperature range that is best for yours depends on the species being kept. Few are able to tolerate temperatures above 78°F (25.5°C) for long, with most needing to be kept somewhere between 50°F (10.0°C) and 65°F (18.3°C). It's crucial to use an accurate thermometer for temperature readings. Avoid the commonly available "stick-on" thermometer strips designed to adhere to the outside of the tank, because they show the temperature of the glass, and not necessarily that of the environment within. Instead, use a traditional glass thermometer or, even better, a digital one with an external probe. Digital thermometers are available at well-stocked pet stores and electronics stores.

Plastic storage boxes make fine enclosures for many terrestrial species, including tiger salamanders.

A cool basement is the perfect place to keep most salamanders and newts. An air conditioned room can work equally well. Often within a room there is a thermogradient, with cooler temperatures being found near the floor and warmer ones near the ceiling. For this reason, you may find it helpful to keep cool-loving species at ground level rather than on a tall aquarium stand or shelf. If the location where you keep your salamanders and newts

When a soil or mulch substrate becomes waterlogged or spoiled, fungus gnats may develop. These tiny flying insects don't harm newts or salamanders, but they are an annoyance and indicate that the substrate should be replaced immediately.

does not stay within their preferred temperature range, you may need to manipulate the temperature within the enclosure. There are a number of ways to accomplish this.

Cooling Methods

Aquarium Chillers The best permanent method for cooling an aquatic or semi-aquatic setup involves using a device called a chiller. Chillers are bulky and expensive but are the only reliable way to keep water in an enclosure well below the temperature in the room. They can be purchased at aquarium specialty pet stores or from fish supply companies on the Internet.

Cooling Fans and Evaporation When water evaporates, its temperature decreases. By increasing the rate at which water in an enclosure evaporates, you may be able to reduce the temperature within it by several degrees. Sometimes simply replacing a glass cover with a screen one is enough to cool a tank. Other times, it may be helpful to position a small fan above the water in an aquatic or semi-aquatic setup to increase the rate at which water evaporates, decreasing the temperature as a result.

Ice Packs A good way to temporarily cool an enclosure is to use ice packs. Usually used therapeutically for our injured bodies, ice packs can be placed on top of an enclosure on warm days to

The leaf litter in this marbled newt enclosure adds a naturalistic touch and provides the inhabitants with hiding spaces.

reduce the temperature within it by several degrees. For extended periods of time, multiple packs can be cycled in and out of the freezer and placed onto the cover. This method works well for aquatic, semi-aquatic, and terrestrial arrangements. You can also experiment by placing ice cubes made of chlorine-free water into filters to cool aquatic areas, but take care not to drop the temperature too quickly using this method.

Turning Off Filters and Lights Electrical devices produce heat, so simply turning off those in contact with your salamander or newt's environment can decrease the temperature. Lights in particular can be quite wasteful in the amount of heat they produce, so on warm days of the year or during emergencies, shut them off to cool an enclosure.

Lighting

Salamanders and newts are secretive animals that prefer dim conditions. Unlike some reptiles, they do not require UVB lighting in order to live well in captivity. In fact, in simple setups lighting is not required provided there is indirect light in the room that provides a photoperiod of 10 to 12 hours a day.

While your tailed comrades do not need lighting, if you grow plants in their enclosure the plants will need light. A single fluorescent tube running the length of the tank is all that's needed if using common houseplants in a terrestrial or semi-aquatic setup. This is also usually sufficient for growing a layer of floating vegetation in aquatic environments. If you are designing a planted aquarium, then it's best to use two to four fluorescent bulbs. Compact fluorescent lighting is an even better choice, though it may not be suitable for all setups because of the amount of heat produced. If you use intense lighting like this to grow plants, ensure that there are dark caves and shelters that allow your salamanders or newts to move out of view—and plan to grow a layer of floating plants to filter out some light.

Dicamptodon tenebrosus

Chapter 3

Feeding

Whether you're watching a tiger salamander scarf down a whole nightcrawler or a tiny fire-bellied newt inhale bloodworms, feeding captive amphibians is an exciting part of their care. The voracious predatory appetite of many newts counters their typical cute and endearing appearance, while seeing a nightmarish siren swallow a small fish can turn a person's initial repulsion into fascination and respect. In order to witness this behavior, you must understand your amphibians' dietary requirements. Some foods can be used often, while others are best given as occasional treats. Provide your newts and salamanders with the appropriate diet and you'll be able to enjoy their feeding behavior for years to come.

Feeding

What food you feed depends on the species of salamander or newt you keep. Terrestrial caudates generally eat live invertebrates of a suitable size, with their diet in captivity consisting of worms, insect larvae, crickets, and other small, soft-bodied creatures. Aquatic and semi-aquatic species are easier to feed because they regularly accept thawed frozen and freeze-dried fish foods in addition to live foods. Thoroughly research the dietary requirements of the species you plan to keep so that you understand their specific needs.

How often you offer food is dependent on the species, age of the animal, and the temperature at which it's kept. Most adult newts and salamanders live well when they're fed two to three times a week. When exposed to cool conditions, their metabolism slows and it may be necessary to feed only every five to seven days. This, of course, all depends on how much food you offer at each feeding. If you feed heavily one day, tone it down the next time you feed. Feeding too much or too often leads to obesity, a common and serious health problem in captive amphibians, so do your best to regulate feedings appropriately. Feed young caudates and larvae daily, skipping a feeding only once in a while.

In addition to feeding the right amount of food, it's also important to provide a variety of different foods for your amphibians. Wild caudates feed on many different foods, and in captivity it's nearly impossible to duplicate this. Provide as much variety as you can to help ensure nutritional requirements are met. While one or two food items may become the staple diet, mix in others every few feedings and never rely solely on just one food.

Feed not only your newts or salamanders well, but also their live foods. Often feeders purchased from pet stores or bait shops have been starved and are not very nutritious. Bulk them up on the appropriate food at least several days prior to feeding them to your amphibians so that their nutritional content is restored.

All salamanders are predators and will eat just about anything—including other salamanders—they can fit into their mouths.

Commonly Available Foods

Many different foods are available for captive newts and salamanders. You can find a handful of good ones at the local pet store. Bait and sporting good stores are also a good place to find worms, spikes (fly larvae), and other healthy caudate meals. If keeping a number of newts and salamanders that prefer live foods, you may find it best to order food in bulk directly from specialty feeder insect companies. These can be located on the Internet.

Worms

Slimy and legless, true worms are a perfect food for newts and salamanders. Many accept worms from forceps, coming out from hiding to investigate the dangling pink morsel that awaits them. Rather than feed in this time-consuming way, you may find it easier to place worms into a shallow feeding dish for terrestrial species so that they do not burrow into the substrate, evading your hungry salamander. Tossing a few worms into the water for aquatic and semi-aquatic species also works well.

Nightcrawlers Only the largest newts and salamanders are able to swallow entire fully-grown nightcrawlers (*Lumbricus terrestris*), but when cut into pieces these worms are perfect for nearly all species. They can be used as the main dietary component for many caudates. Keep nightcrawlers in the refrigerator, where the temperature stays between 35 and 40°F (2 and 4°C). The nutritional content of nightcrawlers depends a great deal on the soil they are kept on. It's best to transfer nightcrawlers from the cup they are sold in to a larger storage container with several inches of top soil.

Leaf Worms Though not as easy to obtain as nightcrawlers, leaf worms (*Lumbricus rubellus*) are an ideal food source because of their moderate size and high nutritional value. They can be purchased at some bait stores, especially those in the Midwest United States. They also can be cultured without too much trouble. To start your worm colony, fill a plastic storage container with several inches (7.6 cm) of soil and partially composted leaves (maple leaves work well). Add worms. You will need to replenish the leaves as they are broken down. Leaf worms will live and breed prolifically in this container, providing a reliable source of home-grown food for your newts and salamanders. Keep leaf worms warmer than nightcrawlers, between 40 and 60°F (4 and 16°C). If you cannot find a place to purchase leaf worms locally, check with bait suppliers on the Internet.

Vacation Feeding

If you're going out of town for more than a week or two, it's a good idea to find someone to stop by and feed your salamanders and newts. Although adult caudates can go without food for quite a while, regular small feedings are best. Do not put excess food in a cage before leaving, because uneaten food in aquatic setups and stray feeder insects in terrestrial ones both can cause problems.

Red Worms The worm species *Eisenia foetida* (sometimes placed in the genus *Bimastrus*), popularly known variously as red worm, red wriggler, dung worm, and manure worm among other things, is small and easy to obtain from bait shops and some specialty pet stores. There is some controversy regarding their suitability for use as food because their coelomic fluids may be toxic to amphibians and other animals. Though many use them as food with success, consider using other worms most of the time.

Fire salamander eating an earthworm. Most salamanders accept various worms, and they make a good staple diet.

Blackworms Live blackworms (*Lumbriculus variegatus*) are rarely refused by aquatic and semi-aquatic species, and are a great way to get picky eaters started. To feed them to your amphibians, simply drop a small glob of the uniquely gross worms into the water portion of the tank and watch your newts or salamanders quickly come out from hiding to eat them. Blackworms are able to live for extended periods of time in an aquarium, allowing your amphibians to graze on them as they are hungry. Blackworms can be purchased at tropical fish stores and should be kept in the refrigerator. It's important to rinse through them with cool water once or twice a day in order to aerate the water and remove dead worms. Once they have been rinsed, pour excess water out so that the water remains shallow for good gas exchange. Blackworms have largely superseded tubifex worms, once the staple live fish food, in availability in pet shops in many places.

Insect Larvae

A variety of different beetles, moths, and flies are cultured commercially for their larvae. Few are suitable for frequent use, but feeding them occasionally is a good way to vary your caudate's diet. Offer them in a shallow dish or with forceps.

Mealworms The larvae of darkling beetles (*Tenebrio* sp.), called mealworms, can be used occasionally to feed some salamanders. They have a hard exoskeleton, which can be difficult for amphibians to digest, so feed mealworms only in small quantities. Keep them on bran, flour, or oats, and with a slice of sweet potato or apple for moisture. When refrigerated, mealworms will last for long periods of time before pupating into beetles.

Superworms Superworms are bigger than mealworms. Also called king mealworms, they are the larvae of *Zophobas* spp. beetles. For most newts and salamanders they are too large to comfortably swallow, and because of their hard exoskeleton they may be difficult to digest. They also are high in fat. Feed superworms sparingly to larger salamanders or not at all.

Wax Worms Greater wax moth (*Galleria mellonella*) larvae are a soft-bodied, easily obtained food and are good to use occasionally for variety. They are high in fat and should not be fed too frequently or obesity may result. To prolong their larval stage, you can keep them in the refrigerator on wood shavings or other packaging they are sold in. Because of their specialized diet, wax worms are difficult to gut load; you should feed them out soon after purchase.

Fly Larvae Two kinds of fly larvae are regularly available. At bait stores, the larvae of the bluebottle fly (*Calliphora vomitoria*) are sold as "spikes" and work great as occasional treats. They pupate very fast at room temperature, the result being annoying insects fully capable of flying around your house, so take care to keep the larvae in the refrigerator. The second type of fly larvae that is readily available is that of the black soldier fly (*Hermetia illucens*). Sold as "phoenix worms" by pet stores and specialty feeder insect companies, they are a good food to use occasionally. Keep phoenix worms at room temperature.

Silkworms Nutritious and available in several sizes, the larvae of the silkmoth (*Bombyx mori*) are a good choice to feed periodically. You can purchase them from feeder insect companies on the Internet and occasionally from herp specialty pet stores. In order to keep them alive they must be fed a special silkworm diet and kept warm, between 75 and 80°F (24 and 27°C).

Superworms are somewhat hard to digest, but it is fine to feed them to your salamanders occasionally. This eastern tiger salamander seems to enjoy them.

Flightless Fruit Flies

Young newts and salamanders need tiny food; flightless fruit flies are a good option. Selectively bred so that they are no longer capable of flying, they are easy to culture at home or to purchase from feeder insect and biological supply companies. Some specialty pet stores also sell flightless fruit flies. Two species are regularly available. At around 1/8 inch (0.3 cm), *Drosophila hydei* is the larger of the two. The other commonly available

Anorexic Amphibians

There are many reasons why newts or salamanders may refuse to eat. Sometimes it is related to their health or the environment they're kept in. Other times they refuse food because the wrong kind is offered. Try live foods if your amphibian isn't feeding, because the movement usually initiates a feeding response. Chopped worms and blackworms are particularly useful for getting picky eaters started.

fruit fly, *D. melanogaster*, stays about half that size. Although flightless, fruit flies can still climb well and have a tendency to quickly crawl up and out of a cage once dumped inside. To slow them down, lightly coat them in a powdered calcium or vitamin supplement. Another good option is to place a small slice of apple or orange into the enclosure to attract the flies, preventing them from crawling up and out of the cage.

Crickets

Along with worms, crickets (usually *Acheta domestica*) can be used to form the staple diet of terrestrial newts and salamanders. They are readily available from pet stores in several sizes. It's best to keep crickets for at least several days prior to feeding them to your amphibians in order to restore their nutritional content. Commercially prepared cricket diets, flake fish food, dry rice baby cereal, and dog food can all be fed to crickets, along with fresh fruits and vegetables like oranges, apples, sweet potatoes, yams, carrots, squash, grapes, and dark leafy greens. Crickets are prone to drowning in water dishes, so instead provide a moist sponge for water or simply feed moist foods. You can keep crickets in small aquariums, garbage cans, or ventilated plastic containers. Whichever option you choose, ensure it stays warm, always above 70°F (21°C).

Never feed more crickets than your salamander or newt can eat within a couple of hours. Crickets that are allowed to roam a cage for several days have been known to nibble on amphibians, turning the predator into prey. The resulting small wounds can lead to infection.

Wild-Caught Invertebrates

A great way to add variety to the diet of captive newts and salamanders is to use food collected from the wild. By sifting through leaf compost, you can collect slugs, grubs, worms, pill bugs, and other useful food items. You can place handfuls of moist leaf compost into a kitchen strainer suspended above a bucket to get these critters out, shaking the compost slightly. Placing a low-wattage light bulb above the strainer can help, encouraging the invertebrates within the leaves to migrate towards the bottom to avoid the heat and light. Running a fine mesh net through a grassy field is another way to get food, capturing field crickets, katydids, and spiders in the process. For aquatic caudates, netting through the water of a local pond can yield good results. Live daphnia, mosquito larvae, large copepods, and other tasty aquatic organisms can be collected.

It's important to understand the risks involved with wild-caught food items prior to collecting them. Pesticides and other harmful chemicals are a large concern, so never collect near farmland or agricultural activity. Parasites also inevitably will be transferred from the wild-caught food to your slimy pets, so weigh this against the benefits of collecting food for your caudates prior to running outside with a net. Use discretion in collecting food from the wild.

Feeder Fish

A variety of live feeder fish is available at pet stores. These work well as occasional treats for aquatic species. Certain terrestrial caudates, like eastern tiger salamanders (*Ambystoma tigrinum*), have also been known to eat live fish from their water source in a cage. The suitability of using feeder fish as food depends largely on the species of fish being used. Guppies are one of the better choices. Avoid goldfish because they are high in fat and can be quite messy if uneaten. Use feeder fish only now and then, relying more heavily on foods like worms and crickets. It's also important to note that it's possible to introduce diseases to captive caudates through using feeder fish as food, so consider this before feeding them to your newts or salamanders.

Mice

Large caudates like axolotls (*A. mexicanum*), tiger salamanders (*A. mavortium* and *A. tigrinum*), and the two-toed amphiuma (*Amphiuma means*) will eat mice. These rodents can be purchased frozen at pet stores and then thawed in warm water before being offered. Few salamanders are able to consume adult mice, so it's often necessary to use young hairless ones, commonly called "pinkies." Feed mice to salamanders only occasionally, because feeding too often leads to obesity and other health problems.

Aquatic and semi-aquatic salamanders (crocodile newt in this photo) usually accept blackworms, bloodworms, and similar fare.

Fish Foods and Commercially Prepared Diets

Many aquatic and semi-aquatic newts and salamanders accept commercially prepared diets. This makes feeding them easy. Unfortunately, the nutritional value of these diets is rarely as high as that of live foods, so it works best to feed prepared diets in between live feedings so that you meet your pet's nutritional requirements.

Worm feeders sold for feeding tropical fish work well for feeding aquatic worms to larval salamanders, such as this larval northern crested newt.

Pellets There are several pellet diets available for aquatic amphibians. Some aquatic newts and salamanders also accept those designed for turtles or fish. While a few species can be maintained almost solely on pellets, it's best to use other foods in conjunction with these diets. Many newts and salamanders show little to no interest in pellets, and if this is the case, other food options will need to be explored.

Freeze-Dried Tubifex and Bloodworms In the fish department of pet stores, you can find cans of freeze-dried tubifex worms and bloodworms. Some aquatic newts and salamanders greedily consume these foods, while others seem to hold off for fresher food items. Freeze-dried foods are not as healthful as frozen or live foods, so it's best to skip over these convenient canned diets for something a little more nutritional. They also can foul the water easily if overfed, so use them sparingly.

Frozen Fish Foods Perhaps the best non-living food to try feeding aquatic and semi-aquatic caudates comes frozen. Normally used for feeding tropical fish, many different types of

Fish Quarantine

Feeder fish are notorious for carrying a variety of parasites and diseases, which could potentially be harmful to your newts or salamanders. For this reason, it's best to have an aquarium setup specifically for feeder fish. You can then keep the fish in this tank for several weeks or months to help ensure their health prior to feeding them to your amphibians. You may even consider breeding them yourself, though this may not necessarily ensure the fish are disease-free.

frozen invertebrates are sold prepackaged at fish specialty pet stores. Particularly good options to use include bloodworms, white mosquito larvae, daphnia (for young or small newts only), and mysis shrimp. Frozen brine shrimp and beefheart are also regularly available and eaten by some aquatic amphibians but are best used in moderation. Thaw frozen foods in a small container of water before feeding them to your amphibians.

Large species, such as this barred tiger salamander, will eat pinky mice, but offering mice too often can make your pets obese.

Vitamin and Mineral Supplements

A particularly important part of feeding your newts and salamanders involves supplementing their food with the appropriate vitamins and minerals. The foods used to feed captive caudates are not nutritionally balanced, and even when caudates are fed a varied diet, nutritional deficiencies can result if multivitamin and calcium supplements are not used. Powdered supplements designed to be coated onto crickets, worms, and other food items can be purchased at pet stores. Usually two separate supplements are needed; one that contains calcium and vitamin D3, and another that is a general multivitamin supplement.

How often you use a supplement depends on many factors. If feeding your salamanders and newts two or three times a week, lightly dust their food items in a calcium or vitamin supplement every other feeding, alternating between the two supplements. When feeding less frequently, it may be best to supplement more heavily at each feeding. Growing young newts and salamanders can have each daily feeding coated in the appropriate vitamin or calcium powder. Feeding supplemented food items to aquatic caudates can be difficult because powdered supplements wash off in water. The slimy coating of worms, however, retains some powdered supplements underwater, and worms are a good way to get the right vitamins and minerals into aquatic animals.

Some aquatic species, such as axolotls, may eat pelleted diets, but it is a good idea to offer live food regularly.

Mesotriton alpestris

Chapter 4

Breeding Newts and Salamanders

The breeding strategies of newts and salamanders are fascinating to observe. Intricate courtship rituals involve dance-like maneuvers, with males rubbing pheromone-secreting glands on females or fanning their tails in an eye-catching display. Raising the resulting larvae is an enjoyable experience, as the tiny gilled amphibians hatch from eggs and transform into voracious aquatic predators, eventually completing metamorphosis and appearing as miniature adults. Arguably more important than simply watching this occur is documenting your observations and sharing them with others. Only a handful of newts and salamanders are bred regularly in captivity, and many species have yet to be bred under captive conditions. Developing a breeding project for one of the many underappreciated caudates can be a groundbreaking new experience that you can record and share with others.

In order to breed newts and salamanders, you must meet two requirements. First, you need a sexually mature male and female; second, you must provide the correct conditions to encourage breeding behavior. The former is often the easier part.

Sexing

How males and females can be distinguished from each other is species dependent. Some caudates are easily sexed, and several of the guidelines below can be applied. Others are best sexed during the breeding season, when their bodies change and a clear difference can be seen between the sexes. There are also species that are difficult or impossible to sex, and if working with one of these amphibians you may need to pay attention to their behavior when breeding occurs to determine who is who.

Cloacal Size

The best way to determine the sex of your salamanders or newts is by examining their underside. Males of many species have an enlarged cloaca (the opening of their urinary, intestinal, and genital tracts). It appears as a bulge between the hind limbs. In certain species the cloaca swells during the breeding season, while in others the difference between males and females is clear year-round. The degree to which it is enlarged is dependent on species, and in some caudates there is no difference in the external appearance between the cloaca of males and females.

Body Structure

Female caudates typically have a larger, more robust body structure. In contrast, males are generally smaller and more streamlined in appearance. This is best seen when two of the opposite sex are placed next to each other. Using body structure as a way to determine the sex of a caudate is not reliable and does not hold true for all species. Instead, use it in combination with other methods.

In most species of salamander, the female is larger and more robust than the male, illustrated here in marbled salamanders.

Color

In some species males develop flashy coloration during the breeding season. While their sex remains unrevealed throughout most of the year, iridescent blues, purples, and even reds appear when they are ready to spawn. These colors usually develop in combination with other physical changes.

Nuptial Pads

Darkly colored sponge-like fleshy bumps appear on the limbs and/or feet of many male caudates during the breeding season. Called nuptial pads, these bumps help male newts grasp females while breeding. The presence of nuptial pads is species dependent, and not all males develop them.

Mental Gland

On many male lungless salamanders (Plethodontidae), a gland called the mental gland can be seen at the tip of the chin. These round or elongated glands secrete pheromones that are rubbed onto females during courtship. In certain male salamanders this gland is large and obvious, and by comparing the chins of a group of salamanders that exhibit this physical characteristic you can distinguish between sexes.

Changing Appearance

The physical appearance of many male newts changes when they are ready to breed. Some develop impressive crested dorsal areas, nuptial pads, brightly colored tails, and a different skin texture. In these species the males and females are often indistinguishable when not in breeding condition.

Breeding

The breeding strategies of some caudates are not well known, while those of others have been thoroughly documented. For most newts and salamanders, fertilization occurs internally through the use of a spermatophore. Males secrete this capsule of reproductive cells after an often intricate courtship ritual. Females essentially pick it up with their cloaca, where eggs are then fertilized. In the giant salamanders (Cryptobranchidae) and certain Asian species, there are no spermatophores; fertilization occurs externally during oviposition. Many different places can serve as egg-laying sites, depending on species. These include aquatic vegetation, the underside of submerged rocks, in moist leaf litter on the forest floor, or near the edge of water in piles of moss. Aquatic predatory larvae hatch from eggs, though in certain species the larvae develop within eggs on land and terrestrial salamanders break free several weeks or months down the line.

Seasonal Cycles

Seasonal changes typically encourage breeding in salamanders and newts. The severity of these seasonal changes required for breeding depends on the species and their native habitat.

The mating embrace of amphibians is called amplexus, seen here in eastern newts.

Many from temperate regions breed when the first rains of spring arrive, venturing in large numbers to temporary ponds. Others spawn in the fall, with the eggs or larvae overwintering. In contrast, the salamanders from tropical and subtropical regions often breed throughout the year. To breed newts and salamanders in captivity, it's usually necessary to replicate the seasonal changes that stimulate your particular species to reproduce in the wild.

Manipulating temperature is one of the most important parts of triggering breeding behavior in captive caudates. A cool period of several weeks or months may be needed. Following this, you can warm up your potential breeders. It's important that you modify their care during these temperature changes so that they remain healthy. As temperatures cool, the metabolism of newts and salamanders slows. In response, feed smaller quantities of food less frequently.

The availability of water is also important for breeding newts and salamanders in captivity. Terrestrial species that breed alongside streams or migrate to ponds need to be moved from their terrestrial setup to a semi-aquatic one during the breeding season. Semi-aquatic and fully aquatic species can also have their available water manipulated, with higher water levels being provided during simulated spring and summer months and lower levels being offered in the winter. You might also consider experimenting with heightened humidity levels during spring and summer months for terrestrial species, increasing it by misting their enclosure with water each day.

In addition to changing the temperature and water availability, you may find it helpful to modify your caudate's photoperiod. Provide longer hours of light during warmer times of the year and less as they are cooled off for an artificial winter. It's also worth experimenting with light intensity, providing less intense light during winter months.

Strategies for Recreating Seasons in Captivity

If you live in a temperate region, the temperature fluctuations that naturally occur inside your house may be enough to promote breeding. To emphasize the seasons, you can move your amphibians to different parts of the house. The floor of a cool basement in winter can lower the temperature within an enclosure considerably. You might also consider moving your newts or salamanders to the garage or other enclosed spot out-doors if temperatures are within a safe range. After several weeks or months of keeping their cage on the basement floor or in the garage, you can move it back to a warmer area of the house to recreate spring and summer months. Temperature increases should be gradual to avoid temperature shock. Use an accurate thermometer to monitor the temperature in the cage and ensure that it stays within a safe range. Consider keeping a record of the temperatures in a notebook for future reference.

Refrigeration You can use a refrigerator to cool caudates in the winter. House them in a storage container or small aquarium containing several inches of moist soil and leaf litter. In the refrigerator, temperatures can remain as low as 35°F (1.7°C) for many species. With these cold temperatures, their metabolism slows considerably and they require little to no food. It's important that newts and salamanders are gradually cooled and well prepared to overwinter in this way. Several weeks to a month prior to placing them in the fridge, begin cooling their normal enclosure by moving it to a cooler area of the house or garage as outlined above.

Make sure your caudates have a good weight and are healthy before exposing them to these harsh conditions. Weak, unhealthy, or malnourished newts and salamanders can deteriorate quickly when cycled through cold temperatures in captivity. If one of your cau-dates is in less than perfect health, do not cool it this year.

No Changes Needed

While some salaman-ders and newts require fairly intense seasonal vari-ations to breed in captivity, others may spawn on their own without any change in care on your part. It's not uncommon for this to occur with some lungless salamanders or certain aquatic species like the axolotl (*Ambystoma mexi-canum*). Some newts and salamanders may also

Two Japanese fire-bellied newt eggs on an anacharis leaf. Live plants make good egg deposition sites.

Competing Males

Some people report that when there are more than two males to each female in a breeding group, a successful spawning is less likely, possibly because of the increased competition between males. For best results, pair off newts and salamanders to their own enclosures. For certain species it may be helpful to keep the sexes separate except during the breeding season.

reproduce on their own in response to fluctuations in temperature and water availability that you did not intend. Many rooms cool during winter months, and if the tank of a semi-aquatic species is neglected, the water level will drop. After a water change and in combination with warmer conditions in the room the amphibians are kept in, you might observe mating behavior the following day.

Egg Deposition Sites

Female salamanders and newts deposit their eggs on a variety of surfaces. Some cages may offer a suitable place to do so without modification, and the female will lay eggs in a large mass underwater or on cage furnishings. In other situations you may need to add plants, smooth-sided caves, dark depressions, or rock ledges so that oviposition can take place.

Many newts deposit eggs individually on aquatic plant leaves, which they then fold over each egg, creating a sort of egg taco. Provide appropriate aquatic plants, such as anacharis (*Elodea densa*), for these species. Less picky newts may use artificial plants or even strips of thin plastic tied together underwater. Other species lay clusters of eggs around submerged sticks, rocks, or roots, and still others prefer aquatic caves for egg deposition sites, with broken flower pots being suitable in captivity.

Some terrestrial caudates, most notably certain plethodontids, do not deposit their eggs within water. Red-backed salamanders (*Plethodon cinereus* and *P. serratus*) often attach their eggs to the ceiling of small burrows or rotted logs. Other species deposit them in a

A setup for Danube crested newts (*Triturus dobrogicus*). Thin strips of plastic serve as egg-laying sites.

small cluster underground. For these salamanders, offer dark moist caves and depressions for them to breed within, such as sections of PVC plastic pipe submerged into substrate, tightly curled dried leaves, or dark crevices created with corkbark slabs.

Caring for Larvae

If they have been fertilized, you will notice development in eggs within several days. To prevent eggs from being disturbed by parents, it's best to remove them from the enclosure. The larvae hatch between one and four weeks after the eggs are laid. This time period depends largely on the species and the temperatures the eggs are exposed to. Larvae remain motionless the first few days after they break free from the egg. Initially they do not require food but instead live off their yolk sacs.

You can raise larvae in fully cycled aquariums or in simplistic aquatic setups as described in the housing chapter. If you use a cover, choose a screen one to allow good oxygen exchange. It's also important to keep the water level shallow for this same reason, particularly during the first week or two. A sponge filter can be used for filtration, but it is best turned on only once larvae have matured and are moving about the aquarium. Using a bare bottom is advantageous because you can easily siphon excess food and other waste out of the tank using a section of tubing or turkey baster. This should be done regularly, sometimes daily if the enclosure is heavily stocked with larvae. Replace water that is removed while siphoning out waste with water of the same temperature.

Newt and salamander larvae are excellent predators, and they require tiny live foods at first. As they mature they often accept thawed frozen fish food. You can purchase brine shrimp hatching kits at pet stores, and larvae rarely refuse the tiny freshly hatched brine shrimp. Another good food option is live daphnia. Biological supply companies and certain fish food suppliers on the Internet offer these crustaceans. Culturing daphnia provides an excellent home-grown food source. Whiteworms are also a good option but are labor-intensive to culture. You may be able to locate starter cultures through local aquarium societies or

Eggs of the two-toed amphiuma. The embryos are visible inside.

A simple setup for raising salamander larvae. The bare bottom makes cleaning the enclosure easy.

online from fish food suppliers. In addition to these foods, you can also offer chopped blackworms purchased from pet stores. Large larvae accept pieces of nightcrawlers and leaf worms.

Feed larvae once or twice a day, but in small amounts to avoid fouling the water. If live daphnia or blackworms are used, they often live within an aquarium for days to weeks at a time if uneaten.

Metamorphosis

The physical appearance of larvae changes as they mature. Their legs become stronger and more supportive, and their skin texture and color may change. Finally, tail fins start to shrink. When you notice these changes, it is time to move terrestrial and semi-aquatic species to an enclosure with access to land.

An aquarium or plastic storage container with shallow water is an ideal setup for metamorphosing larvae. Add clumps of Java moss protruding from the water's surface or floating corkbark flats for access to land. Alternatively, gravel can be used for a land area. Slope it

Caring Caudates

Certain salamanders and newts guard their eggs, defending them from potential threats and caring for them as they

Female marbled salamander guarding her eggs.

develop. Males of the fully aquatic hellbender (*Cryptobranchus alleganiensis*) remain with their eggs for weeks, even helping oxygenate the water surrounding them. In other salamanders, such as the marbled salamander (*Ambystoma opacum*), it is the female who stays with the eggs, gently nudging and turning them as they develop.

Culturing Daphnia

Daphnia inhabit freshwater systems, mainly being planktonic and feeding on unicellular algae, bacteria, and detritus. Often called water fleas, they are a good food to feed larvae. To culture them, you need an aquarium, several empty clear bottles, and a fine net.

Start by filling the clear bottles with water. Place the bottles in an area that receives intense light. Soon planktonic algae will grow and the water will turn green—this is what you feed the daphnia. Once algae cultures have been setup, purchase several hundred daphnia from a biological supply company. Place them in an aquarium (it does not need to be heated or filtered). Pour in green water as needed to feed the daphnia, refilling the bottles with water before they are completely emptied of algae. Daphnia also eat yeast. Thoroughly mix yeast into water and then pour it into the aquarium to feed daphnia. Use a fine net to capture daphnia to feed to your larvae.

Daphnia cultures tend to "boom" and then "crash," and they can be somewhat unreliable. For this reason it is helpful to have several daphnia cultures set up.

gradually towards one end to form a ramp for morphing caudates to crawl up. Drowning is of particular concern for terrestrial species, so make certain land areas are easy to access. Aquatic and certain semi-aquatic species do not need to climb out of the water upon metamorphosis. Instead, they can be left in their existing aquarium.

Newt and salamander larvae are highly cannibalistic. Prevent them from making a snack out of their siblings by sorting them by size, housing larvae that grow faster than others with similarly large individuals. You may even consider raising larvae individually in separate cups if you have only a few. Keeping larvae well fed may also help reduce cannibalism.

Surplus Salamanders

Hundreds of captive-bred newts and salamanders can be produced during a single breeding season. To avoid introducing foreign pathogens to native wild amphibian populations, never release captive-bred individuals into the wild. You can instead give or sell them to other passionate caudate enthusiasts who can be located through herpetological societies or on the Internet. You might also be able to find a specialty pet store that is willing to buy them.

Taricha torosa

Chapter 5

Health Care

I f cared for properly, most captive newts and salamanders live 10 to 20 years, but this is dependent on the species involved. Certain species can live longer. A Japanese giant salamander (*Andrias japonicus*) at the Amsterdam Zoo survived over 50 years in captivity! You can help pet newts or salamanders live a long, healthy life by understanding the common health problems they face. These include bacterial and fungal infections, wounds and abrasions, and nutritional deficiencies. Learn about the causes of these problems to prevent them from developing, and about the symptoms so you are prepared if they arise.

Veterinarians

Amphibian-savvy veterinarians are difficult to come by, but locating one and forming a good relationship with him or her is important. Many illnesses are impossible to diagnose without a veterinarian's assistance, and the knowledge and resources veterinarians have access to prove invaluable in the captive care of amphibians. Vets also have access to helpful prescription medications, which are needed to treat certain diseases. Keep the phone number of a local vet clinic on hand so you're prepared if the health of your amphibian deteriorates.

Quarantine

Quarantine is an important and simple process that prevents the spread of disease among your salamanders and newts. It's the first step to take if you notice one of your pets deteriorating in health. Also, always quarantine newly acquired animals, especially if they are going into the same enclosure as ones already in your care. Quarantine newly acquired animals for a period of 30 days or more, and introduce them to others in your care only if they appear healthy after this time.

A good quarantine procedure completely isolates a new or unhealthy animal from others. You can use a small plastic storage container or extra aquarium for housing, but keep the cage setup simple so that monitoring the potentially unhealthy animal will be easy. Terrestrial species can have their quarantine enclosure lined with moist paper towels, while aquatic species can be kept on a bare bottom with a piece of PVC plastic pipe or other easily cleaned hide spot. In this quarantine enclosure you can medicate an unhealthy amphibian as advised by a veterinarian, or if quarantining a newly acquired caudate, sim-

With proper care newts and salamanders can be long-lived pets; for example, fire salamanders have been known to live more than 20 years.

ply observe it for several weeks or months to ensure it is healthy before introducing it to others in your care. Always care for quarantined animals after you have finished maintaining others, and wash your hands thoroughly before and after their care. Doing so prevents spreading infection from the quarantined animals to your established ones.

Stress

Stress is often the underlying cause contributing to the poor health of captive amphibians. It weakens the immune system, allowing diseases to take over. By keeping stress to a minimum, the immune system of your newts or salamanders will stay

A simple quarantine setup for terrestrial salamanders.

strong and they will be less susceptible to health problems. Handling, fluctuating temperatures, irregular water quality, aggressive tankmates, overcrowding, excess feeder insects, and being moved to a new cage all can stress a newt or salamander. A particularly stressful time is when you first acquire your caudates, and during this period it's important that you monitor their health carefully.

Heat Stress

Heat stress is one of the most common problems in captive newts and salamanders. When kept above their preferred temperature range, many caudates rapidly deteriorate in health. Unusual restless behavior and anorexia often accompany heightened temperatures. Terrestrial species sometimes soak continuously in their water dish when overheated, and aquatic ones may constantly float near the water's surface. In some cases kidney damage can result, and several days following a period of high temperatures your newt or salamander may become bloated and swell with fluids. Even when none of the symptoms of heat stress are present, warm temperatures can allow other health problems to develop, so keep a close eye on the thermometer in the tank and ensure that it stays cool.

Bacterial Infections

Bacterial infections are difficult to detect in captive amphibians until it is too late to treat them. For this reason it's essential that you do not create conditions favorable for bacteria to develop. A stressed salamander kept on a spoiled substrate and at elevated temperatures is a good candidate for a bacterial infection. Temperature fluctuations and poor water quality can also contribute to the development of bacterial infections.

Infection usually begins as a result of a compromised immune system. Lethargy, anorexia, tremors, patchy coloration, clouded eyes, burst blood vessels, and paralysis are all symptoms of a bacterial infection. Localized infections may show themselves as swelling or discoloration, especially around a wound or sore. Antibiotics can be a successful treatment, but first a veterinarian should determine the particular type of infection. Some people report successfully using fish medications (such as nitrofurazone and furazolidone) from pet stores to treat aquatic and semi-aquatic caudates, but it's a safer option to get in touch with a vet, because using medications without knowing what type of bacterial infection is present can be risky.

Fungal Infections

Fungal infections are a serious concern. They often are noticed as white fuzz or a cotton-like growth on aquatic species and larvae. Other types of fungal infections do not look like the common fuzzy or white-colored growth mentioned above. Localized discoloration, particularly around a wound, or swollen areas on the body can also indicate the presence of a fungal infection. Fungal infections regularly accompany other health problems and generally affect immune-suppressed caudates suffering from poor care. If you notice what appears to be a fungal infection, double check the temperature and water quality. A veterinarian can diagnose and recommend treatment for the specific type of fungal infection affecting your newt or salamander. A general treatment effective in some situations involves using a saline solution and soaking the amphibian in this for a period of time each day or dabbing it on an infected area with a sterile cotton swab. Whether this is suitable for your salamander or

Bloat

Bloated caudates look as though they have been pumped full of a gas or liquid, with a swollen abdomen, throat, and/or limbs. Aquatic species may have trouble swimming as a result. Bloat is a symptom that can be brought about by many ailments, including temperature stress, kidney damage, poor water quality, and bacterial infections. If you notice bloating, take your amphibian to a qualified veterinarian. The vet may be able to determine the cause of it and find a suitable treatment.

newt and the concentration of the solution should be determined by a veterinarian.

Parasites

A wide variety of small (often microscopic) parasitic creatures can infest your captive newts and salamanders. In fact, it's likely most captive amphibians harbor parasites. Different types of parasites live in different parts of newts and salamanders. They can inhabit the digestive tract, muscles, lungs, blood, and skin. Often parasites do not present a large problem for captive amphibians provided that the host is in good health and not exposed to stressful conditions. Typically, immune-suppressed caudates end up with serious parasite problems, and in these situations parasites reach elevated levels that push an already weakened amphibian over the edge.

Keep your newts and salamanders within the appropriate environmental conditions and avoid stressful situations so that parasites do not become a problem. Two common symptoms of a parasite infection include lethargy and loss of weight. External parasites are typically noticed as tiny dots or grayish areas on aquatic caudates or, more often, on larvae. If any of these symptoms are noticed, contact a veterinarian who can determine whether a parasite is the culprit. The vet may

A bacterial infection is the probable cause of the swollen front feet on this fire-bellied newt.

ask you to bring in a fecal sample if internal parasites are suspected, which can be collected by moving the newt or salamander to a simple setup consisting of moist paper towels or a bare-bottom aquarium.

Abrasions, Wounds, and Trauma

Sharp or unstable cage items, aggressive tankmates, and shipping accidents can injure newts and salamanders. Treat wounds quickly to prevent infections from developing. Triple-

Death and Necropsies

While most salamanders and newts can live over a decade in captivity, some don't survive this long and succumb to a disease or illness early on. If you are unsure what caused the death of your salamander or newt, a veterinarian may be able to determine this. Finding out the cause of death is important if you have other amphibians at home. Be in touch with a veterinarian if you notice a health problem develop. If your salamander or newt dies as a result, you can bring the body in for a necropsy to determine the cause of death. Refrigerate the body to slow decomposition, or freeze it if it will be more than a day before you can bring it to the vet.

antibiotic ointment can be dabbed onto small abrasions once a day with good results. Alternatively, use a cotton swab to apply a saline solution on the wound a couple of times each day. Whichever option you use, contact a vet if the injury does not start to improve after several days. Serious trauma may require amputation or euthanasia.

Nutritional Deficiencies and Imbalances

Little is known about the nutritional requirements of amphibians when compared to what we know about those of other vertebrates. Nutritional deficiencies or imbalances in amphibians may be more common than we think. A varied diet is the key to avoiding nutritional problems. It's also important to complement a varied diet with a high-quality multivitamin supplement. Nutritional deficiencies develop over the long term and can be difficult to correct once they are present, so do your best to prevent them. Symptoms of nutritional deficiencies are varied but can include lethargy, paralysis, uncoordinated movements (ataxia), and tremors. A diet lacking in important vitamins or minerals can also lead to other health problems.

Metabolic Bone Disease

Though not as common in caudates as in many reptiles, metabolic bone disease is still a concern. It results when there is an imbalance in calcium, vitamin D3, or phosphorus. Symptoms include lethargy, irregular posture, bone fractures (kinked spine, tail, etc.), and muscle tremors. Crickets, blackworms, and other commonly available feeders contain high levels of phosphorus, an element that in amphibians inhibits calcium intake. If feeding a diet largely composed of these food items, it's crucial to supplement them frequently with a phosphorus-free calcium supplement. Leaf worms and nightcrawlers are better balanced in their calcium and phosphorus content, though this is largely dependent on the composition of the soil they are kept on. If worms are used as the main dietary component, calcium supplementation will not be needed as often.

Impaction

Newts and salamanders are effective predators, but they are not always very graceful in capturing prey. Sometimes along with the food they eat comes some of the substrate they are kept on. If they are unable to pass this, it can become lodged inside of their digestive tract and cause an impaction. Gravel and small bark chippings are notorious for causing impactions in amphibians, though even soils and fine sands occasionally cause problems if too much is swallowed. Surgery is required to fix serious blockages, but other times the objects pass on their own. Abdominal bloating and lethargy are signs of an impaction. Move your newt or salamander to a substrate of moist paper towels or a bare-bottom setup if you

Note the distended mouth and throat of this warty newt (*Paramesotriton* sp.), likely the result of an infection.

notice that a sizable rock or large quantities of gravel have been swallowed, and check their feces to see if this passes over the following days. If it doesn't and abdominal bloating is noticed, contact a veterinarian.

Stout Salamanders

Captive newts and salamanders seem to have an endless stomach, continually eating food as it's offered, showing no sign of becoming full. It's easy to overfeed them because of this, which can lead to obesity. An obese newt or salamander looks pudgy, with a round, overfed abdomen. Put your salamander or newt on a diet by reducing both the frequency and quantity with which you feed in order to correct this.

Cynops orientalis

Chapter 6

Fire-Bellied Newts: the Genus *Cynops*

Well deserving of the common name fire-bellied newt, all seven members of the genus *Cynops* display an eye-catching fiery orange ventral side. This attractive pattern, coupled with this newt's widespread availability, has made the Chinese fire-bellied newt (*Cynops orientalis*) one of the most popular pet amphibians. The other *Cynops* species are less frequently encountered in the pet trade but are worthy of your attention. Get to better know the Chinese fire-bellied newt (*C. orientalis*) and you too will likely become interested in the other members of the genus *Cynops*.

Chinese fire-bellied newts are among the most commonly available species. They are quite hardy when given proper husbandry.

Description of Species

The fire-bellied newt genus *Cynops* contains seven described species. Two of the seven (*C. ensicauda* and *C. pyrrhogaster*) are native to Japan, with the other five being found in China.

All are small to medium-size semi-aquatic newts with bright red or orange bellies. One *Cynops* species, *C. wolterstorffi*, is thought to be extinct.

Chinese Fire-Bellied Newt (*Cynops orientalis*)

Small in size, the Chinese fire-bellied newt can grow to a length of 4 inches (10.2 cm), but often stays smaller. Dorsally, adults are smooth and seal-brown to black in color. This contrasts sharply with their bright vermilion ventral sides patterned in irregular black blotches. *C. orientalis* has a large range throughout southeast China, where it lives in a variety of habitats, from forest ponds and pools to rice paddies and seepages in degraded habitat. Heavily imported for the pet trade, the Chinese fire-bellied newt is perhaps the most commonly available caudate.

Japanese Fire-bellied Newt (*Cynops pyrrhogaster*)

Japanese fire-bellied newts are capable of growing to slightly over 5 inches (12.7 cm) in total length. In comparison to the Chinese fire-bellied newt, their dorsal color is lighter, a chocolate brown, while underneath they are a similar mottled orange. They also have a rougher skin texture. There are six separate subspecies of *C. pyrrhogaster*, differing in morphology and distribution. They are all native to Japan, where they live among grassland and forest pools, ponds, and streams.

Blue-Tailed Fire-Bellied Newt (*Cynops cyanurus*)

Similar in size to the Chinese fire-bellied newt, the blue-tailed fire-bellied newt differs in color and pattern. During the breeding season, males develop a stunning blue luster that gives their usual dark dorsal side a ghostly appearance. A dot is always present just to the back of the eye, and this spot is the same color as this newt's beautifully patterned carrot-orange belly. In the wild, blue-tailed fire-bellied newts are found at relatively high altitudes in a portion of southwest China, where they live and breed in ponds and rice paddies.

Sword-Tailed Newt (*Cynops ensicauda*)

Elegantly patterned, the sword-tailed newt is considered by some to be the most attractive member of the genus. The subspecies *C. ensicauda popei* displays irregular white to golden dorsal blotches on the typically darkened *Cynops* back. Ventrally, the coloration of *C. ensicauda* is variable, from solid orange to dark brown. The sword-tailed newt is the largest *Cynops* species, with some individuals reaching 6.5 inches (16.5 cm) in total length. They have a restricted distribution in forest streams and ponds in Japan, where their existence is threatened by habitat destruction.

Sword-tailed newts grow larger than Chinese fire-bellied newts and should be housed in bigger enclosures. They also are more terrestrial, so you should provide them with a slightly bigger land area.

False Fire-bellies

Several other newts with orange ventral sides are found for sale under the common name of fire-bellied newt. These include the paddle-tailed newts (*Pachytriton* spp.) and warty newts (*Paramesotriton* spp.). Sometimes these species are masqueraded under the name giant fire-bellied newts. Their care is different from that of *Cynops* species, and they should not be kept with them.

Other Fire-bellied Newts

Three other species from China complete the genus *Cynops* but, because of their status as endangered species, are not available in the trade. One of the three, *C. wolterstorffi*, has not been seen since the late 1970s and is presumed extinct. The other two, *C. chenggongensis* and *C. orphicus*, have extremely restricted distributions. Habitat destruction and pollution continue to threaten their remaining populations.

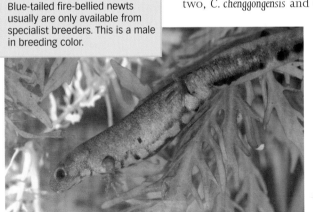

Blue-tailed fire-bellied newts usually are only available from specialist breeders. This is a male in breeding color.

Captive Care

Care for the popular Chinese fire-bellied newt is outlined below, with the differences for other species noted where appropriate.

Acquisition

The Chinese fire-bellied newt is regularly offered for sale through pet stores. Though easy to locate, the species is not always kept in appropriate conditions, so it can be troublesome to find healthy individuals. When purchasing one, first inspect its environment. It should not be housed with other species, so avoid purchasing individuals heavily stocked with other semi-aquatic amphibians, such as fire-bellied toads (*Bombina orientalis*), which may have introduced pathogens foreign to the newts. Also note the temperature at which they're being kept if possible. Fire-bellied newts exposed to warm conditions at pet stores sometimes develop health problems a few weeks down the line. Finally, look at the individual newts. Avoid those that have obvious health problems, and ensure yours has clear eyes, smooth skin, and is not missing digits or parts of its tail. Sometimes captive-bred Chinese fire-bellied newts and their larvae can be located through dedicated newt breeders, and this is by far the best way to acquire them.

The back of a sword-tailed newt displays irregular pale blotches, making for an unusual and beautiful terrarium pet.

Besides *C. orientalis*, *Cynops* species are not often seen at pet stores. To find these other fire-bellied newts, get in touch with a local herpetological society or search the Internet for a newt breeder.

Housing

Chinese fire-bellied newts are simple to house. They are not aggressive toward one another and can be kept in groups. A standard 10-gallon (38-l) aquarium is suitable for a trio, but you should consider using a larger tank; with a greater volume of water, the system will be more stable and easier to maintain. A 30-gallon aquarium (113.6-l) provides enough room to keep a group of five to eight newts. Make certain the aquarium cover you choose is secure, because fire-bellied newts are notoriously good at scaling glass to escape their captive homes.

Chinese fire-bellied newts are quite flexible regarding the way their semi-aquatic environment is set up in captivity. You can use a simple bare bottom, with a secure pile of rocks protruding from the water in a corner, and a couple of artificial plants for cover. More elaborate setups also work. Perhaps the most attractive way to house fire-bellied newts is in a densely planted aquarium. Emergent vegetation, clumps of Java moss, and a gently sloping piece of driftwood jutting out from the water can provide access to land. Offer a water depth in excess of 8 inches (20.3 cm). Sponge filters are the preferred filtration method for small newts like fire-bellies, but submersible power filters can be used instead if the output is diffused so that the current is weak.

While adult Chinese fire-bellied newts rarely leave the water, young newts sometimes prefer a terrestrial enclosure. If your juvenile newts regularly stray from the water in a semi-aquatic setup, you can house them in a separate enclosure on a soil substrate with leaves and bark for shelter. You can move them back to a semi-aquatic setup once they mature. It should be noted that, although it is more natural for juvenile fire-bellied newts, a terrestrial period is rarely required.

Temperature

A critically important part of Chinese fire-bellied newt care is the temperature at which they're kept. You can maintain the tank permanently between 65°F (18.3°C) and 70°F (21.1°C) for convenience, but seasonally varying the temperature may be beneficial. A drop to between 50°F (10°C) and 60°F (15.6°C) for several months of the year works well. Never expose Chinese fire-bellied newts to temperatures above 75°F (24°C). Other *Cynops* species should be kept within a similar temperature range. It's worth noting that the sword-tailed newt tolerates warm temperatures well, with those near 78°F (25.6°C) not presenting a problem.

Diet

Chinese fire-bellied newts accept a variety of food items. Adults greedily feed on small leaf worms, chopped nightcrawlers, blackworms, fly larvae, and wax worms, which are best dropped into the water where the newts most often feed. Thawed frozen foods such as bloodworms and tubifex worms are also regularly accepted by fire-bellied newts. Some individuals eat prepared pelleted diets, though many others refuse them. You can offer food three times a week when keeping these newts near room temperature, bumping back to every five days during particularly cool times of the year.

Female blue-tailed fire-bellied newt wandering in her planted aquarium. The fire-bellies do well in aquatic to semi-aquatic setups.

Land-Dwelling Newts

Unhealthy adult Chinese fire-bellied newts may spend considerable amounts of time on land. Check the temperature, water quality, and other environmental conditions if you notice that your newt avoids the water. If these conditions are all in line, your newt may just be going through a normal terrestrial period in its life, particularly if it is a juvenile.

It's not uncommon for recently acquired Chinese fire-bellied newts to refuse food, especially if they have been overstocked or kept at unusually warm temperatures at a pet store or dealer. Once in your care, they may continue to refuse to eat, especially if offered nothing but non-living foods. To coax a new fire-belly to feed, try blackworms or chopped earthworms, both of which are eagerly consumed by most newts. Take care not to feed too heavily during this initial acclimation period, and keep temperatures within the appropriate range to avoid health problems from developing.

Breeding

Chinese fire-bellied newts are not difficult to breed in captivity. Unfortunately, few people focus efforts to do so, because imported newts from China are readily available. The other three species of *Cynops* are also deserving of breeding efforts, particularly the blue-tailed fire-bellied newt and sword-tailed newt, both of which are infrequently seen for sale.

Sexing

During the breeding season, males are easily distinguished from females because of their swollen cloacas. Additionally, male Chinese fire-bellied newts are typically smaller than females and have a slightly shorter tail in comparison to their body length. Sexing the other available *Cynops* species is similar.

Conditioning

Breeding is normally initiated by rising temperatures following an extended cool period. By keeping the temperature in the tank between 50°F (10°C) and 60°F (15.6°C), the newts will presume it is winter. You can keep them at these low temperatures for several months. It's often easiest to do so during cool months of the year, as the temperature in your house decreases. Following winter, the temperature can increase to 70°F (21.1°C), and if fed heavily during this time, females swell with eggs. At excessively warm temperatures, breeding does not occur. Sometimes, natural fluctuations in temperature coupled with a water change or other stimuli can spark breeding behavior.

Males interested in breeding follow females around the tank, sometimes fanning their tails at them or nipping at them. Females deposit eggs individually on the leaves of aquatic plants, commonly using anacharis (*Elodea densa*) to do so in captivity. One female can deposit over two hundred eggs, though they usually produce fewer. Eggs develop into larvae in around three weeks. Eggs should be moved to a separate aquarium for the best yield.

Care of Larvae and Young Newts

Black and gray larvae hatch from eggs at a small size. They should be kept in water with little to no current and cared for in a similar manner as described in the breeding chapter (Chapter 4). Most accept the same food items as adults, but these foods must be finely chopped or crushed to accommodate the larvae's smaller mouths. You can also feed daphnia and freshly hatched live brine shrimp to larvae.

It takes several months to half a year for larvae to complete metamorphosis. At this point, move them to a new enclosure with shallow water (1 to 3 inches [2.5 to 7.6 cm]) that has easy access to land. There are two approaches to keeping young Chinese fire-bellied newts. The first allows them to live their life terrestrially, as they probably do in the wild, later returning them to a more aquatic setup as adults. This approach works well, but feeding can be difficult, with hatchling crickets, flightless fruit flies, and very finely chopped leaf worms or black-worms forming their diet. You may instead keep juvenile Chinese fire-bellied newts aquatically to make feeding easier. Use shallow water to prevent drowning and a bare bottom to facilitate easy cleanup. Their diet can include the same foods as for adults. Within one to three years the young newts reach maturity.

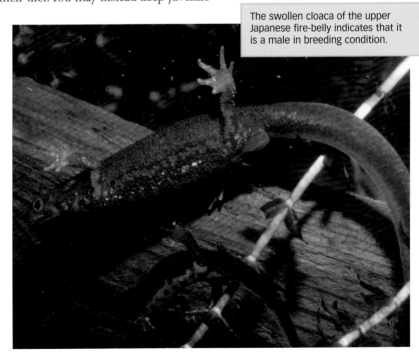

The swollen cloaca of the upper Japanese fire-belly indicates that it is a male in breeding condition.

Ambystoma mavortium nebulosum

Chapter 7

Axolotls and Mole Salamanders: the Genus *Ambystoma*

Some of the most popular salamanders to keep in captivity are those of the family Ambystomidae, commonly called mole salamanders. These mainly terrestrial and often secretive caudates make superb pets when provided with the proper care. Their tremendous appetites combine with their adorable, seemingly smiling faces, both adding to their appeal. Captive breeding is hardly ever achieved, making them worth the attention of dedicated newt and salamander enthusiasts in search of a new challenge. Learn about their care in captivity as well as their natural history and you will likely become as passionate about these fascinating salamanders as I am.

There are many more mole salamanders than can be covered in a hobbyist care guide. Here are a few species you may encounter in the field: (top to bottom) California tiger salamander (*Ambystoma californiense*), flatwoods salamander (*A. cingulatum*), southern long-toed salamander (*A. macrodactylum sigillatum*).

Natural History

The genus *Ambystoma* contains 32 species. They are commonly called mole salamanders because most spend their adult lives in burrows, which they either excavate themselves or take over once another similarly sized animal has moved on. Ambystomids range throughout North America, with the species being evenly divided up between Mexico and the United States. The range of several also extends north to Canada. Breeding for most takes place in the spring, after the first rains arrive. During this time of year, hundreds of individuals in a population emerge from their holes and migrate together toward water to spawn. Many breed in temporary ponds. By using these short-term water sources, they avoid predation by fish and other aquatic animals.

Description of Species

Below are descriptions of five commonly kept *Ambystoma* species. The maintenance methods outlined in this chapter can be applied to most other mole salamanders, but take care to research the best way to keep the particular species you're interested in to make sure it's a match.

Tiger Salamander (*Ambystoma mavortium*)

Perhaps the largest terrestrial salamander in the world, the tiger salamander can grow close to 14 inches (35.6 cm) in total length. Most stay smaller than this, but all have a robust body structure with an appetite to match. There are five recognized subspecies of the tiger salamander, each differing in appearance and distribution. In terms of coloration, the five subspecies are diverse, ranging from warm gray with darkened blotches to elegant black and mustard yellow striping to russet coated in deep black swirls and spots. Tiger salamanders have a large range, the largest of all mole salamanders, with populations being found throughout the western United States, into Canada, and as far south as Mexico.

Eastern Tiger Salamander (*Ambystoma tigrinum*)

Formerly the eastern tiger salamander was considered as multiple subspecies of *A. tigrinum*. Most now accept that there are two different species, and a few of the former *A. tigrinum* subspecies have been given full species status. This leaves the eastern tiger salamander with a patchy distribution throughout the eastern United States, extending west only as far as Minnesota and Texas. Eastern tiger salamanders occupy a variety of habitats, including forests, marshes, and grasslands surrounding bodies of water. They are variable in appearance but generally are a dark brown to olive color, mottled or blotched in black or gray. Although capable of growing to 13 inches (33 cm) in total length, most individuals stay smaller.

A brightly marked tiger salamander from Thomas County, Kansas. This species is highly variable in color and pattern.

Salamanders as Fish Bait

The gilled larvae of tiger salamanders, usually called waterdogs, are frequently offered for sale as fishing bait in some areas of the United States. Rarely are they given good care in bait shops, so be especially careful if you purchase tiger salamander larvae there; definitely check for signs of infection and other health problems.

Spotted Salamander (*Ambystoma maculatum*)

Well dressed for its common name, the spotted salamander is polka-dotted in yellow, gold, or occasionally orange. Backing these vibrant spots is dark gray to black, fading ventrally. Spotted salamanders range in size as adults from 6 inches (15.2 cm) to 9.75 inches (24.8 cm), living a secretive existence in forests near vernal pools, where they breed en masse during early spring. Spotted salamanders have a large range throughout most of the eastern United States and parts of southern Canada. In captivity they are notoriously shy, more so than the other mole salamanders mentioned in this chapter, but are also fairly hardy and have been documented to live over 20 years under captive conditions.

Eastern tiger salamander (left) next to a blotched tiger salamander (*A. mavoritum melanostictum*) for comparison.

Marbled Salamander (*Ambystoma opacum*)

A truly striking amphibian, the marbled salamander's dorsal side is banded in silver stripes, sometimes with an almost blue hue. Underlying these stylish markings is black, which usually forms a circular pattern between the silver bands. Though they have a big, stocky body, in terms of length marbled salamanders are small, measuring between 3.5 inches (9 cm) and 5 inches (12.7 cm). Found throughout the eastern United States, from New Hampshire to eastern Texas, they are completely terrestrial and live within forests, often near small bodies of water.

Marbled salamander reproduction is fascinating It stands out among the different reproductive patterns of the mole salamanders. Females lay eggs during the fall and do so terrestrially in depressions on the forest floor near ponds or ditches. As rain fills these dry forest beds with water, eggs hatch and larvae emerge, completing metamorphosis before the depressions dry.

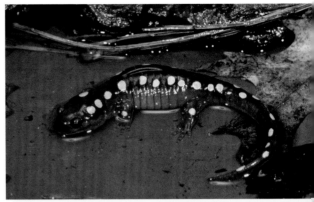

Normal and albino spotted salamanders. This species emerges from hibernation very early in the spring, often when there is still snow on the ground.

Axolotl (*Ambystoma mexicanum*)

The only regularly available neotenic mole salamander is the axolotl. These alien-like gilled amphibians have been used extensively for research and as a result have found their way into the pet trade. Adults measure around 10 inches (25.4 cm) in length, though some grow larger. Captive breeding has brought about some peculiar color morphs, with albino, leucistic, gold, piebald, and melanistic individuals being more commonly available than dark gray wild types. I'm often reminded of the Stay-Puft marshmallow man from the movie *Ghostbusters* while looking at the fat white and eerily grinning face of a leucistic axolotl. While axolotls are fairly common in captivity, their wild populations are in trouble.

Axolotls are only known from a single lake near Mexico City, which has now been drained. The remaining canals and waterways around this empty lake are where the last wild axolotls live.

Captive Care

Though secretive, mole salamanders are enjoyable caudates to keep. The enthusiasm with which they feed is a pleasure to observe and often the highlight of their care. In order to view this, they must be acquired in good health, kept within a suitable environment, and fed an appropriate diet.

Acquisition

Mole salamanders can be acquired a number of ways. Pet stores are the most common place to purchase them. They are not regularly stocked and instead show up seasonally, usually collected for the pet trade during the spring breeding season. When buying a mole salamander or any other salamander for that matter, always examine both the animal and its environment. Avoid salamanders with clouded eyes, unusual patchy coloration, or those that are behaving abnormally (wandering about the cage, resting in the open, continually soaking in the water dish, etc.)

Often a better option than purchasing a mole salamander is collecting one. If you live with-

Axolotls are bred in several color morphs. This is the golden form.

in the range of the species you want to work with, consider spending some time outside in search of a salamander. By doing so, you avoid supporting the commercial collection of salamanders and get to enjoy the experience of being outdoors looking for amphibians. Mole salamanders are best located after a rainstorm, particularly in the

Melantistic form of the marbled salamander found near Aiken, South Carolina.

spring, when adults move from their burrows to breed. This time of year it's also possible to collect salamander eggs or larvae instead of adults, an even better option. Check with local laws before capturing a wild animal. Some such collections may be completely illegal or may at the least require a permit.

Housing

Living a quiet terrestrial life within burrows much of the year, mole salamanders do not require complex housing. Instead, their cage setup should reflect their fossorial lifestyle, providing them with suitable places to dig and burrow beneath.

You can use both aquariums and plastic storage containers to house mole salamanders. Outfit aquariums with a tight-fitting screen cover; if plastic bins are used, drill holes for ventilation. While mole salamanders can be kept together, it's important that they are all a similar size, because cannibalism can occur if smaller individuals are kept with larger ones. Two big tiger salamanders should be provided with a minimum enclosure the length of a 20-gallon (75.7-l) "long" aquari-

A Long-Term Commitment

Never release a salamander that you caught and kept in captivity back into the wild. During its time in your care it may have come in contact with a pathogen that could be harmful to wild amphibians in your area. If you choose to collect a mole salamander, do so only if you intend to keep it for the remainder of its life, remembering that these salamanders may live ten years or longer.

Heat Stress

um, while a pair or trio of the smaller species can be housed in a 10-gallon (38-l) aquarium.

The most important part of housing your ambystomid is the substrate. It must be moisture retentive and safe. Perhaps the easiest substrate to use is moist paper towels. Use multiple layers, first one that coats the bottom of the enclosure and then several others lightly piled around the cage to offer hide spots. These should be changed frequently, sometimes several times a week. If you prefer a more natural appearance, a blend of coconut husk fiber or top soil with cypress mulch works well. I have used this blend with a tiger salamander for more than a decade, changing it as needed several times a year. It's crucial to maintain a good moisture gradient throughout this soil and mulch blend, with the top layer or one side of the cage remaining drier than the other. While some people house mole salamanders on a substrate of gravel, that is not a good option; it does not hold moisture and can cause impactions if accidentally ingested.

Furnish the cage with several pieces of corkbark or driftwood for cover. A comfortable mole salamander will spend most of the time buried under these cage items. You can also place a layer of dried leaves over the substrate for shelter, but make sure that they have been collected from an area free of pesticides or other harmful chemicals. To complete the cage setup, submerge a shallow water dish into the substrate.

Axolotl Housing Unlike terrestrial mole salamanders, axolotls should be kept in aquariums. A standard 20-gallon aquarium (75.7-l) is large enough for two adults. Furnish the aquarium with several hide spots, placed over a bare bottom to facilitate quick partial water changes. If a more natural setup is desired, gravel can be used, but it should be of a large grade to prevent impactions. Perform 15 to 30 percent water changes every one to two weeks, and use a sponge or power filter to capture waste in the water column between water changes.

Temperature and Humidity

In mole salamander burrows it always stays cool. Ideally, their cages should be kept between 60°F (15.6°C) and 72°F (22.2°C), avoiding temperatures in excess of 75°F (24°C). Healthy tiger and marbled salamanders are somewhat tolerant of occasional warm days during which their cage approaches a temperature of 78 to 80°F (25.6 to 26.7°C), although their ability to cope with these hot conditions may depend on where they were collected from. Cool temperatures down to 50°F (10°C) are not a problem.

While humidity is important for many terrestrial amphibians, it is not crucial for keeping mole salamanders, which are constantly in contact with their moist substrate. When mole salamanders are kept in dry rooms, the water in their cages evaporates quickly, and you may find it necessary to pour water onto the substrate several times a week. Alternatively, you can spray the cage with water to bring about temporary increases in moisture and humidity.

Diet

Few moments in the captive care of salamanders surpass the excitement of watching a ferocious tiger salamander take down a full-grown nightcrawler. Mole salamanders are impressive predators, consuming nearly any invertebrate that fits into their mouths. Large species will even feed on newborn mice and other amphibians. Their captive diet should mostly be composed of worms and crickets. For small species like the marbled salamander, large worms can be cut into smaller pieces and offered with forceps or in a dish. Other food items to try in addition to crickets and worms include mealworms, wax worms, fly larvae, silkworms, and large guppies, but these items should not make up the majority of the diet.

Mole salamanders mainly feed at night, though in captivity most can be conditioned to eat during the day. Tiger salamanders in particular rarely refuse food and will even become accustomed to being hand-fed. Feed adult mole salamanders every three to five days, reducing the frequency of feedings when kept at cool temperatures. Several crickets or a worm per salamander at each feeding is usually enough. When crickets or other low-calcium, high-phosphorus feeders are used, coat them in an appropriate calcium supplement.

Breeding Site Fidelity

Most mole salamanders return to the site where they left the water in order to spawn as adults, migrating in large numbers during the spring breeding season. Some amphibian hobbyists speculate it's advantageous to start a captive breeding project with larvae or eggs that have been raised in captivity rather than wild-caught adult animals conditioned to return to their specific breeding site.

Maternal Marbled Salamanders

Unlike other ambystomids, female marbled salamanders incubate their eggs on land, within forest floor depressions near water. They only leave their eggs once the waters of the flood zone in which they have deposited the eggs rise. The resulting offspring return to this same area to breed once they mature.

Additionally, use a high quality multivitamin supplement every few feedings.

Breeding

Of all ambystomids, only the axolotl is bred in captivity with any frequency, often doing so with little stimuli other than fluctuations in temperature that naturally occur in their aquarium. There are also accounts of the marbled salamander breeding in captivity, but this is uncommon. Most other species have never bred under captive conditions. Though in part this may be due to lack of interest, most would attribute the poor captive breeding success of mole salamanders to their strongly seasonal spawning and breeding site fidelity. This is unfortunate, because it leaves the pet trade to rely on commercial collection of wild salamanders. With many species already suffering from habitat destruction and other threats, large-scale collection at certain sites could be harmful to wild populations. For this reason it's well worth your attention to experiment and develop new breeding techniques for ambystomids.

Sexing

Male mole salamanders have an enlarged cloaca, which is best seen when compared to a female's. Maturity for some species can take several years, while others, like the axolotl, are capable of maturing in only six months.

Methods

Those who have bred mole salamanders in captivity usually have done so with large outdoor enclosures or pens, where seasonal changes spark breeding behavior as they do in the wild. Changes in temperature, humidity, and photoperiod all contribute to whether or not breeding takes place. Long, cool winters followed by an increase in temperature and strong rain drive mole salamanders out of their winter holes and to the breeding ponds. By placing animals in the garage or refrigerator for several months and then moving them indoors, eventually transferring them to a semi-aquatic or fully aquatic setup, you may be able to initiate breeding. This method has only rarely worked, and it's worth trying out new approaches to breed mole salamanders in captivity. The use of a rain chamber, similar to those used to breed many frogs, has also been suggested as a means to breed ambystomids following an extended winter cooling.

Wild ambystomids typically lay eggs on underwater objects such as aquatic vegetation or submerged branches, with eggs being deposited either singly, in strings, or small clusters. Females of some species can produce thousands of eggs, though most produce several hundred. The time it takes eggs to hatch into larvae is dependent upon the species and water temperature, but generally larvae emerge between two weeks and one month. The larvae develop over the following months into adult animals, with neoteny being observed in certain populations of the tiger salamander as well as in five other species of mole salamanders.

Care for the larvae is the usual method as described in Chapter 4 of this book. Note that larger ambystomids have sizable larvae. Because of their size they will produce a considerable amount of waste, and if housing a lot of larvae you will want to use a substantial aquarium or other container that holds a large volume of water.

Larval eastern tiger salamander. Unfortunately, the mole salamanders rarely breed in captivity.

Desmognathus monticola

Chapter 8

Lungless Salamanders: the Family Plethodontidae

Containing more than 350 species, the family Plethodontidae holds over two thirds of all caudates. Only a handful of the plethodontids are kept in captivity, but those species display some of the most interesting behavior of all. Some deposit eggs in little clusters suspended from the ceiling of their rotten-log homes. Others secrete glue-like slime from mucous glands in their skin when threatened. Common to all plethodontids is their lack of lungs, with respiration occurring solely through the skin and mouth tissues, hence their common name. This chapter focuses on the care of the lungless salamanders most commonly encountered in the pet trade. The more advanced salamander enthusiast may wish to pursue others less frequently kept. If this is you, take care to document the conditions that you provide for them, because few plethodontids have to this date been worked with in detail.

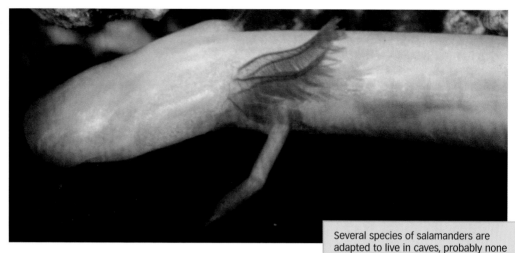

Several species of salamanders are adapted to live in caves, probably none more so than the Georgia blind salamander (*Eurycea wallacei*).

Natural History

Nearly all lungless salamanders are found in the Americas, the only exceptions being Italian cave salamanders (*Speleomantes*) and the recently described Korean crevice salamander (*Karsenia koreana*). Many plethodontids are native to Mesoamerica. Here miniature *Thorius* salamanders and the bizarre suction-cup footed, semi-arboreal *Bolitoglossa* species live. In the eastern United States, a diverse array of plethodontids can also be found, including alien-like cave salamanders (*Eurycea* spp.) and the beautiful red salamander *Pseudotriton ruber*.

Many lungless salamanders inhabit woodlands and forests, often near rocky creeks or streams. Some live a completely terrestrial life, under piles of rotting wood or in thick leaf litter, while others are completely aquatic. Tropical species exist that occupy rainforests, and there are also lizard-like plethodontids that prefer moist rocky outcrops and damp caves.

Lungless salamanders typically have intricate courtship rituals. Males dance around females, periodically rubbing them with pheromone-secreting glands. Reproduction sometimes occurs via direct development, whereby eggs are laid on land and fully formed miniature salamanders hatch out.

Description of Species

Since the focus of this chapter is on a handful of commonly kept plethodontids that are occasionally encountered in the pet trade, we'll have only a handful of genera and species to cover.

Redback Salamanders (*Plethodon cinereus* and *P. serratus*)

Small, with short stubby legs and elongated bodies, redback salamanders are variable in color. Some are dark gray, speckled in silver. A salmon to vermilion stripe runs down the back and through most of the tail. Others are uniformly brownish gray or charcoal, often heavily marked with light flecks or dots. Redback salamanders range in size from 2.5 inches (6.4 cm) to 5.0 inches (12.7 cm) in total length. Northern redback salamanders (*P. cinereus*) have a large range, from Minnesota east through Quebec and New Hampshire. The southern redback (*P. serratus*) is patchily distributed farther south. Both are abundant in forests, where they live a completely terrestrial life in rotten logs, among leaf litter, under stones, and in other damp places.

Palm Salamanders

Sporadically imported and notoriously difficult to keep are two tropical climbing salamanders of the genus *Bolitoglossa*: *B. dofleini* and *B. mexicana*. These funny-looking suction cup-footed caudates are remarkable animals. Both spend a considerable amount of time above ground, taking refuge in water-filled plants during dry parts of the year in Central America. In captivity they require a humid setup, with a relatively dry substrate, climbing areas, and tropical temperatures hovering around 75°F (24°C).

Unfortunately, even professional institutions have rarely been able to keep these two palm salamanders alive for more than a few months. They often appear in good shape initially, only to drop their tails and refuse food several weeks down the line. The chytrid fungus responsible for many amphibian population declines and extinctions has been found in recently imported *Bolitoglossa* as well, and it is suspected to have contributed to their demise in captivity. With this bad reputation, palm salamanders are best left for only the most advanced caudate hobbyist and zoological institution willing to invest the needed money and time in developing a way to acclimate them to captive conditions.

Ecuadorian palm salamander (*B. ecuatoriana*)

The southern redback salamander has a patchy distribution in the southern United States including parts of Missouri, Arkansas, Georgia, and North Carolina.

Two-Lined Salamanders (*Eurycea bislineata* and *E. cirrigera*)

Often with an attractive background color of golden yellow or light amber, two-lined salamanders have two black, sometimes broken, stripes running from their eyes to their tails. Additionally, the dorsum is often speckled heavily in black, creating the appearance of a third dorsal stripe in certain individuals. Small and slender, they range in size from 2.5 inches (6.4 cm) to a maximum of 4.8 inches (12.2 cm). The northern two-lined salamander (E. *bislineata*) ranges from northern Virginia and Ohio up to southern Quebec, while the southern two-lined salamander (E. *cirrigera*) occurs from northern Florida to eastern Illinois.

Redback Color Morphs

Many people separate redback salamanders into two color morphs: "redbacks" and "leadbacks." Redbacks are the familiar striped form, while leadbacks are solid in color. Both occur together in the wild, with intermediately colored individuals also existing.

Both generally live close to water, often at the edge of rocky creeks or springs, where they breed by depositing white egg masses on the underside of submerged rocks.

Slimy Salamanders (*Plethodon glutinosis* and Related Species)

Slimy salamanders are contrastingly colored in black and white. They grow to between 4 and 8.5 inches (10.2 and 21.6 cm) depending on species. There is confusion regarding how many slimy salamanders there are, with some suggesting as many as 13 recognized species composing the P. glutinosis complex. Fitting for their common name, slimy salamanders produce a thick, sticky mucus when threatened, so take care to use wetted gloves if handling them, or even better, a moist net covered with a gloved hand. They range throughout the eastern United States, from New York to Florida, and west to Texas. Here they spend their days under rotted wood and concealed in leaf litter in forested areas, sometimes near moist ravines or floodplains.

Northern two-lined salamanders live on the edges of brooks and streams, but they may wander away from this habitat during wet weather.

Dusky Salamanders (*Desmognathus* spp.)

The dusky salamanders, a semi-aquatic group, are found throughout the eastern United States, with the range of two species extending north to Canada. There are around nine *Desmognathus* species commonly referred to as dusky salamanders, though older literature often places some of these species at the subspecies level. Most mature to a small size of between 3.0 inches (7.6 cm) and 5.0 inches (12.7 cm), though a couple of species are capable of approaching 7 inches (17.8 cm) in total length. Typically, dusky salamanders inhabit cool seepage streams and creeks, where they often spend time in wet rock crevices. They seem to sporadically turn up in the pet trade, but if you live within their range they can be located by turning rocks in suitable habitat.

Lungless Locales

Many of the commonly available lungless salamanders are widespread. Those found for sale in the pet trade are rarely labeled with a collection site. Some species are difficult or impossible to tell apart based on morphological differences alone, so you may never know which species is in your care if you acquire a lungless salamander through a pet store or herp dealer.

Captive Care

The care of the salamanders covered above is relatively undemanding. A number of other plethodontids from eastern North America can be cared for in a similar manner, but you should research the specific microhabitat where the species you're interested in occurs to ensure it is like those of the species described in this chapter. Tropical lungless salamanders, fully-aquatic cave salamanders, and other plethodontids with drastically different behaviors and lifestyles will not survive under the care guidelines given below.

Acquisition

Slimy salamanders, redback salamanders, dusky salamanders, and two-lined salamanders appear in the pet trade from time to time. Some pet stores occasionally stock them or may be able to special-order them for you. Herp dealers or private collectors may be a better source for acquiring these species, but they are not always available. The best way to get a hold of plethodontids is to capture them yourself. In that way you are not supporting the large-scale commercial collection that supplies the pet trade, and you also have the opportunity to observe them in the wild before doing so in captivity. Check with local laws before collecting a salamander, and never release back into the wild a salamander that you collected. Captive breeding has been achieved but is rare, and it's fair to say most lungless salaman-

The small size of redbacks and similar species can make them a challenge to feed.

Pattern and color vary considerably in slimy salamanders. All those in this picture were collected at Lookout Mountain in Georgia.

ders are not available in the form of captive-bred stock. You can change this, being the first to consistently breed the species that most interests you.

Housing

Redback and slimy salamanders are completely terrestrial and do not require standing water in captivity. In contrast, dusky and two-lined salamanders do best when housed in semi-aquatic streamside environments. These two separate approaches to housing are described below.

Housing Redback and Slimy Salamanders
In captivity, any number of terrestrial housing styles can work for redback or slimy salamanders. While redbacks are small and can live comfortably in 2- to 5-gallon (7.6- to 19-l) aquariums or ventilated plastic storage containers of a similar size, slimy salamanders can grow considerably larger and should be kept in an enclosure the size of a 10-gallon (38-l) aquarium. Pay close attention to the sex of the salamanders you're keeping, because males are quite territorial. Males can be kept together successfully, but it's a good idea to provide extra room if you choose to do so. Use a screen cover to prevent escapes.

Moist paper towels are a practical substrate, but you will need to change them often. Top soil, coconut husk fiber, cypress mulch, or a mix of these ingredients can be used for a

Many lungless salamanders mark their territory with scents. Although cleanliness is important, it may also be stressful for territorial lungless salamanders to have their cages cleaned frequently. Doing so disrupts their territories, so clean their enclosures only when necessary.

more natural approach. Whichever you choose, pay close attention to how much moisture it retains. You might consider crumpling up layers of moist paper towels so that near the top the towel remains only slightly moist, while the bottom stays wetter. If a soil or mulch blend is used, you can raise an end of the aquarium slightly so that one side is higher than the other and as a result stays drier.

Within the cage, the only furnishings needed are hide spots. If you house multiple salamanders together, ensure there are enough hiding spots for each individual salamander. Leaf litter, cork-bark flats, loose piles of moss, and prefabricated reptile and amphibian hides are all good options. Paper towels used as a substrate can also form hide spots if crumpled up for salamanders to burrow beneath. Do not provide a dish of standing water. Redback and slimy salamanders can drown in standing water if it is difficult to climb out of.

Housing Two-Lined and Dusky Salamanders

Living in close proximity to water in the wild, two-lined and dusky salamanders need semi-aquatic environments in captivity. You will need to base the size of the land area and depth of the water according to the particular species you keep. For most, you can create a portion of land that takes up somewhere between 20 and 50 percent of the horizontal floor area. The water depth can vary from 1 inch (2.5 cm) to a maximum of 10 inches (25.4 cm). Although two-lined and dusky salamanders can live in small 5- or 10-gallon (19 or 38 l) aquariums, it's advantageous to use larger tanks because the more water you use, the more stable the setup will be. It's also a good idea to provide a slight current using a small

Ouachita dusky salamanders (*D. brimleyorum*) in a rocky semi-aquatic terrarium.

submersible power filter. Diffuse the output with a rock if it seems to be too strong or, even better, use rocks to create somewhat separate pools of water with varying amounts of current.

A good way to create a semi-aquatic environment for your two-lined or dusky salamanders is to use rocks to form a land area. The rocks can be securely stacked in a way that offers crevices both in and out of the water for your cau-dates. Pay attention to the type of rock used, because

Cave salamanders (*Eurycea lucifuga*) in a streamside terrarium.

some can adversely affect water quality. Slate, granite, and quartz are good rocks to use, and you should avoid marble, limestone, and any rock with a metallic shine. Java moss can be draped over rocks to form soft, moist areas for your salamanders to take refuge in. You do not need to use gravel as a substrate, but if you do, make certain the rocks that form the land area are positioned on the bottom of the enclo-sure rather than on the gravel so that they do not shift over time. Perform partial water changes weekly.

Temperature

Like most other salamanders, the plethodontids described in this chapter like it cool. Always avoid temperatures above 75°F (24°C). If the tank reaches warmer temperatures, heat stress may result, and long-term exposure can end in death. Ideally, you should keep their enclosure between 60°F (15.6°C) and 70°F (21.1°C). Drops below this range are usu-ally tolerated well. To provide these moderate temperatures, keep the tank on the floor in an air-conditioned room or in the basement. On warm days, shut off any lights that are on the tank, and in extreme conditions place ice packs on top of the cover or mist the tank with water to bring the temperature down.

Diet

In the wild, an assortment of small invertebrates forms the diet of plethodontids, from millipedes and spiders to aquatic worms and crustaceans. Some even prey on smaller salamanders. Offer captive plethodontids a varied diet. Feed redback salamanders small crickets, chopped leaf worms, flightless fruit flies, and wild-caught food like pillbugs, springtails, and termites. Dusky and two-lined salamanders feed on similar foods but can also be offered blackworms and tubifex worms. You may also be able to wean semi-aquatic species onto thawed frozen foods. Slimy salamanders feed on the usual fare of crickets and worms in captivity but will also eat fly larvae, mealworms, wax worms, and other insect larvae. Offer food two to three times a week, feeding less frequently at cooler temperatures. Use the appropriate vitamin and mineral supplements to prevent nutritional deficiencies from developing.

Similar Does Not Mean the Same

While the housing requirements of certain plethodontids may be similar, different species should not be housed together. Differences in size and competition will undoubtedly lead to problems down the line when multiple species of lungless salamanders are housed together in a small aquarium.

Breeding

Lungless salamanders have some of the most fascinating reproductive behavior of all caudates, but strangely breeding is rarely the focus of those who keep them in captivity. Many plethodontids deposit eggs terrestrially. Females may remain with them until hatching, eating infertile eggs to prevent the egg mass from spoiling. Other plethodontids lay eggs aquatically, sometimes in secretive underwater rock crevices. To breed plethodontids in captivity, it's important to understand the breeding strategy and behavior of the particular species you're working with.

Sexing

The methods used to distinguish male lungless salamanders from females vary depending on species, and sexing some species can be tricky. For the species covered in this chapter, mental glands appear on the chins of the males during the breeding season. Male dusky salamanders can also be told apart by their often longer snout-to-vent length. Sexing females or immature males is a bit more difficult, and sometimes impossible. Developing eggs can be seen through the skin of some gravid females, most notably in two-lined and redback salamanders.

Captive Breeding Strategies

While caudates like the fire salamander (*Salamandra salamandra*) and crested newt (*Triturus cristatus*) have been bred repeatedly in captivity for decades, plethodontids have not been thoroughly worked with. This leaves plenty of opportunity for you to develop new captive breeding techniques. The species discussed in this chapter have bred in captivity, but not consistently—breeding often occurring unintentionally without added stimuli. Regardless, if breeding is your goal, you might consider experimenting by varying photoperiod, temperature, and humidity levels.

In the wild, two-lined salamanders deposit white egg masses aquatically on submerged rocks. In contrast, the other species in this chapter usually lay eggs on land. Slimy salamanders find a secretive location to nest, such as within a rotten log. Redback salamanders suspend their eggs from the ceiling of their moist homes in grape-like clusters. Only six to nine eggs are typically produced at a time. Dusky salamanders look for damp, often muddy, crevices near the small streams where they live to deposit their eggs. Certain dusky salamanders may prefer to submerge their eggs underwater rather than lay them terrestrially at the water's edge. Provide suitable sites for your salamanders to nest in captivity if breeding is your goal. For slimy or redback salamanders, this might mean offering dark caves or simply a loose substrate with moist leaf litter for them to nest in. Two-lined salamanders should have submerged rocks, while you may need to get creative with dusky salamanders and create damp depressions next to water with moist moss or soil suitable for nesting.

Male plethodontids of some species develop protrusions called cirri on their upper lips during the breeding season, as seen on this Blue Ridge two-lined salamander (*E. wilderae*).

Females guard their eggs until they hatch. Poor success has been had raising plethodontid eggs without females to brood them in captivity, so it may be advantageous to leave the eggs with the female until they hatch. While two-lined and dusky salamander eggs hatch into aquatic larvae, slimy and redback salamanders undergo direct development. Out of their eggs hatch little miniature versions of the adults.

Salamandra salmandra

Chapter 9

The Fire Salamander
(Salamandra salamandra)

Highly variable in contrasting suits of black and yellow, orange, or red, the various subspecies of *Salamandra salamandra*, all popularly known as fire salamanders, are indisputably among the most striking amphibians in the pet trade. They live well in captivity, being both hardy and easily cared for provided they are kept cool. Fire salamanders are desirable for first-time caudate keepers because of their ease of care and also for more advanced hobbyists because of their fascinating reproductive strategies. With over a dozen separate subspecies of fire salamanders, all differing in color, pattern, and distribution, there are plenty of incredible *Salamandra* to choose from.

Natural History

Although the brightly colored fire salamanders looks as if they would fit well into a lushly flowering tropical rainforest, they actually are native to temperate Europe. There their range spans from Spain to Bulgaria, where they spend their days hiding among leaf litter and moss in a variety of moist wooded habitats.

Often they're found near forested streams, and it's in these cool, flowing waters where their fascinating reproductive behavior occurs. Rather than deposit eggs, females drop fully formed larvae into the water after the eggs have hatched inside of them. The subspecies *Salamandra s. bernardezi* and S. s. *fastuosa* from northern Spain even give birth to fully metamorphosed land-dwelling miniatures of themselves. Fire salamanders are nocturnal and hide during the day, only occasionally venturing out at night. It's at this time that they feed on a variety of invertebrates, from spiders and millipedes to snails and slugs.

Two of the subspecies of the fire salamander—*Salamandra salamandra fatuosa* is shown—give birth to terrestrial young that look like miniature adults.

Description

Fire salamanders are relatively large terrestrial animals as salamanders go. Some individuals from southern parts of their range reach 12 inches in length (30.5 cm), although most grow only slightly larger than half that size. They have a stout body structure, with short, thickset legs. Adding to this robust appearance are two bulging parotoid glands at the base of their head, from which unpleasant secretions can ooze if the salamander feels threatened. Additional poison glands run along the sides of their bodies. While potentially dangerous to small mammalian predators, the toxic secretions of fire salamanders are not a great concern for keepers. Regardless, avoid handling fire salamanders and always wash your hands immediately after contact with a salamander to play it safe.

A background color of jet black is dominant on all subspecies, over which swirls, dots, blotches, or stripes are patterned. These can range in color from golden yellow to pumpkin orange, with populations from Spain displaying a mixture of these colors overlaid in deep red. Some individuals, most notably those of S. s. *gigliolii* and S. s. *fastuosa*, have less black on them, occasionally being almost solid yellow.

Taxonomists have divided the fire salamander into thirteen subspecies based on molecular and morphological differences. Each subspecies occurs in a geographically separate area, and although individuals vary in appearance, most have distinct colors and patterns associated with them. Some have called these taxa subpopulations rather than subspecies, and in future years it is likely that fire salamander taxonomy will change as more research is carried out. Only a couple of subspecies are commonly available, but most others can be located by talking with dedicated newt and salamander hobbyists. *S. s. salamandra* and *S. s. terrestris* are two of the most common in the trade.

Captive Care

Beautifully patterned in contrasting colors and with a personable demeanor, the appeal of fire salamanders is unquestionable. They are a superb first salamander to keep because their care is relatively undemanding, captive-bred stock is available, and they are hardy. Provide them with cool temperatures, a moist environment, and a suitable bug-filled diet and you will enjoy your fire salamander for decades.

Acquisition

While some might say fire salamanders are not as easy to come by as they were years

Fire Salamander Subspecies

S. s. alfredschmidti—several river valleys in northern Spain

S. s. almanzoris—Sierra de Grados of central Spain

S. s. bejarae—central Spain, but not in the Sierra de Grados

S. s. bernardezi—extreme northwest Spain (Asturias and Spanish Galicia)

S. s. beschkovi—southwestern Bulgaria (Pirin Mountains)

S. s. crespoi—Sierra de Monchique of southern Portugal

S. s. fastuosa—western Pyrenees, around the border of France and Spain

S. s. gallaica—Most of Portugal and northern Spain

S. s. gigliolii—Italy

S. s. longirostris—extreme southern Spain

S. s. morenica—southern Spain (Sierra Morenica)

S. s. salamandra—widespread, from Romania west through the Alps

S. s. terrestris—France, Belgium, and Luxembourg

Fire salamanders have large parotoid glands containing copious amounts of defensive toxins.

ago, you still can locate them from a variety of sources. The best place to get one is from a breeder. Fire salamanders are one of a handful of caudates that are bred regularly in captivity. By searching the Internet, talking with people at a local herpetological society, or attending a herp show, you can locate healthy captive-bred *Salamandra*. Specialty pet stores also occasionally stock fire salamanders, though these are often wild-caught adults. Whichever route you go, be certain that the individual salamander you pick is healthy. Avoid fire salamanders that are resting out in the open or wandering about their cage, because healthy individuals are shy and conceal themselves under hide spots most of the time. Also pass up fire salamanders that are housed in inappropriately warm enclosures; they may develop health problems once in your care.

Housing

Fire salamanders are simple to house. A standard 15-gallon (57-l) aquarium is large enough for a pair. Use a screen cover to offer ventilation. Fire salamanders are not prone to escaping, but the cover will keep in stray feeder insects.

A substrate of coconut husk fiber, top soil, finely milled cypress mulch, or a blend of these ingredients works well. You can use moist paper towels for juveniles so that they can be monitored easily. Keep the substrate moist but not wet or waterlogged.

The substrate should also stay loosely packed so that your salamanders can dig in it. While fire salamanders don't generally excavate deep burrows the way mole salamanders do, they often wedge themselves under cage furnishings by pushing substrate out of the way. To accommodate this behavior, place several pieces of corkbark, driftwood, or flat stones over the substrate for shelter. Commercially available reptile and amphibian hide spots also work well. Hardy live plants like pothos and small ferns can be grown if lighting is provided, but they are not necessary to keep fire salamanders happy and healthy. To complete the setup, add a small, shallow water dish. Fire salamanders rarely soak in this, but it's a good idea to have water available for them anyway.

A more aesthetically pleasing housing method is employed by some keepers and many zoos. First, several inches (7 cm or so) of small-grade gravel are placed in the bottom of the tank. In one corner, the depth of the gravel is decreased and held back by stones or heavy driftwood. Over the gravel, a divider like fiberglass window screening is placed, followed by several inches of a soil mixture, leaving the corner with shallow gravel exposed. The tank is then planted with live plants and attractive mosses. As water drains through the soil it accumulates in the drainage layer of gravel and, as a result, makes water available in the corner of the tank. Partial water changes are performed with a siphon and should be done regularly. This housing style is best reserved for large enclosures, but the result is a beautifully detailed woodland terrarium that requires minimal maintenance on your part provided you don't stock it densely.

Shy Salamanders

Although they have flashy coloration, fire salamanders are shy creatures. Provide them with plenty of hide spots in captivity so they feel secure.

Temperature and Humidity

Wild fire salamanders experience a wide range of temperatures, often retreating in dormancy during cold winter months. Down under logs and beneath the leaf litter of the forest floor, temperatures always remain cool, even on warm summer days. You must duplicate this in captivity in order for your salamander to remain healthy. Keep the cage between 50°F (10°C) and 65°F (18.3°C) most of the time.

House fire salamanders in cool, humid woodland terraria with plenty of cover.

The Fire Salamander (Salamandra salamandra)

This species tolerates temperatures approaching 32°F (0°C) in captivity. If the temperature is allowed to drop this low, the change should be gradual. Never allow the temperature to rise above 70°F (21.1°C) or the salamanders will suffer from heat stress.

Fire salamanders seek out cool, humid hide spots during the day. The humidity level in their enclosure can vary a great deal as long as these moist retreats are available to them. Pay close attention to the moisture content of the substrate. This is more of a concern than the ambient humidity level. Spraying the cage with water will increase the humidity during dry times of the year and also decrease the temperature in the cage on especially warm days.

Diet

Like all other caudates, fire salamanders are predators, feeding on a variety of live invertebrates. In captivity their diet can be composed largely of crickets and worms. Some people also report permanently maintaining fire salamanders on a diet of mealworms supplemented with the appropriate vitamin and calcium supplements, but because of mealworms' hard exoskeleton and high fat content it's best to use them sparingly. Other occasional feeders to offer include silkworms, wax worms, fly larvae, slugs, and snails. Feed three or four crickets or a couple of worms every three days, decreasing both the quantity and frequency fed during cool times of the year. Other feeders can be mixed in periodically. It's easy to overfeed fire salamanders because of their greedy appetite, so cut down on feedings if your salamander appears obese. Use high-quality powdered supplements to lightly coat food items every couple of feedings.

Fire salamanders are nocturnal, and although most accept food during the day, it's often better to feed at night when they are ready to eat.

Breeding

Breeding typically takes place during the fall. Males in breeding condition constantly follow other salamanders around at night, looking for a potential mate. If they are successful, gestation takes several months, with the female depositing larvae in shallow water during the spring. It's not particularly difficult to coax your salamanders to do this in captivity, but

Cool Alternatives

If you can not maintain a cool environment for a fire salamander, it's best to look into keeping a more temperature-tolerant species. Consider a marbled salamander or a sword-tailed newt, both of which can withstand warmer temperatures and display equally impressive coloration.

Not all fire salamanders are brightly colored. This is a particularly dull *S. salamandra bernardezi*, one of the subspecies that has terrestrial young.

first you must start with at least a pair of salamanders and then provide them with conditions favorable for breeding.

Sexing

Mature fire salamanders are easily sexed. The cloaca of a male appears swollen or enlarged in comparison to that of a female. Additionally, female fire salamanders typically are more robust in appearance. Sexual maturity in captivity occurs when the salamanders are between two and four years old. Juveniles cannot be sexed.

Conditioning

Breeding can occur in captivity as a result of fluctuations in temperature that naturally occur in the room they're kept, but you will likely find it helpful to exaggerate these temperature extremes to promote reproduction. Subspecies and populations from more

The Fire Salamander (Salamandra salamandra)   **101**

Most of the fire salamander subspecies have aquatic larvae; a larval *S. salamandra salamandra* is shown here.

northerly regions of Europe undergo a significant winter cooling. You can replicate this for captive populations by placing their enclosure in a cool area, such as on the basement floor, eventually transferring them to the refrigerator, where they can be maintained at a temperature near 39° F (4°C). At this cool temperature, their metabolism will slow and fire salamanders require little or no food. If you are working with salamanders that come from southern populations, only moderate cooling is needed. In a temperate climate the temperature variations of your house at different times of the year may be adequate conditioning.

Gradually warm up the salamanders following the cool period. Breeding will likely occur during this time. Sometimes breeding takes place in the fall and females are already gravid after a cool winter. Move gravid females to a setup with a shallow and easily accessible water area to deposit larvae in. The nature of the water area is important; if it is too deep or difficult to climb out of, females may drown. Consider placing angled rocks into it to make access in and out easy. Larvae are not deposited all at once, and instead females make repeated trips to the water area over the course of a month or more.

Pond Water

Some people net zooplankton from local ponds for feeding the larvae. Although the dietary variation is good, you run the risk of introducing foreign pathogens and potentially harmful creatures if feeding in this manner.

Care of Larvae and Young Salamanders

As many as 75 larvae may result from a successful breeding, though numbers of around 30 or less are more common. Larvae measure near

S. salamandra terrestris found near Dordogne, France. This is one of the more commonly available subspecies.

0.8 inches (2 cm) in length and have all four limbs along with frilly gills. It's usually best to remove larvae to a separate aquarium, and many keepers find it best to rear them in small separate containers because they can become quite aggressive while feeding. Offer a variety of food to larvae, including live daphnia, chopped earthworms, and blackworms. They also accept thawed frozen fish foods.

Larvae kept within a similar cool temperature range as the adults can take over three months to complete metamorphosis. At warmer temperatures and when offered more food, they will leave the water quickly, in as little as 28 days, although it may be advantageous to keep them cooler so they remain larvae for a longer period of time. As their gills shrink and body structure changes, the larvae will need access to land. Decrease the water depth and provide piles of Java moss or gently sloping rocks that break the water's surface so that they can climb out easily. Drowning is a concern, so monitor metamorphosing fire salamanders carefully.

You can keep freshly morphed fire salamanders in small containers and on a substrate of moist paper towels or soil. Their flashy adult coloration will develop several days following metamorphosis. Feed them well, offering flightless fruit flies, small crickets, and chopped worms supplemented with the appropriate vitamins and calcium.

The Fire Salamander (Salamandra salamandra)

Tylototriton sp.

Chapter 10

Other Newts and Salamanders

Dozens of different newts and salamanders are kept in captivity in addition to the handful of species mentioned in previous chapters. It's impossible to cover them all in this book, but with this chapter I attempt to fill in some of the gaps. The captive care of caudates strongly reflects their natural history. If you have difficulty locating care information about a particular species you're interested in, find reports of their environment and diet in the wild and then duplicate it in captivity.

Female (top) and male (bottom) alpine newts. Like many other aquatic salamanders, alpine newts are more popular in Europe than in the US.

Alpine Newt

The available subspecies of *Mesotriton alpestris*, all of which are generally lumped under the name alpine newt, are a pleasure to keep. Males develop spectacular coloration, being largely iridescent blue-gray dorsally, with black speckles bordering the orange ventral side. To top it off, during the breeding season males develop a contrastingly colored, fin-like dorsal ridge. Females are more subdued in color, being brownish gray with reduced black dotting. Alpine newts stay small, growing to a maximum of 5 inches (12.7 cm) in total length. There are ten subspecies, of which only a few are commonly kept and bred in captivity. They inhabit stagnant to slow-moving water bodies in Europe, from forest ponds to drainage ditches near pastureland. Neotenic populations exist in Bosnia, Slovenia, and Montenegro.

Care

The captive care of alpine newts is uncomplicated. Pet stores and herp dealers rarely stock them, but you can easily locate captive-bred alpine newts through breeders. A standard 15-gallon (56.8-l) aquarium is large enough for four adult newts. It's advantageous to use a larger tank so that there is a greater volume of water, and as a result a more stable aquarium.

Alpine newts only need access to a small land area. This can be accomplished with a floating piece of corkbark, emergent vegetation, or a securely stacked pile of rocks. Offer a water depth in excess of 8 inches (20.3 cm). Avoid filtration that produces a strong current. Sponge filters are the best option, but submersible power filters can also be used if the output is diffused. Keep your alpine newts between 50°F (10°C) and 65°F (18.3°C), avoiding temperatures above 70°F (21.1°C), and feed them live blackworms, chopped terrestrial worms, fly larvae, bloodworms, and tubifex worms.

Breeding

Seasonal changes encourage these newts to breed in captivity. In some situations, fluctuations in temperature within the abovementioned range are enough to induce breeding behavior. If breeding is your goal, though, it's usually best to move your newts to a cool location for the winter to emphasize seasonal changes. They will tolerate temperatures near freezing. After this winter cooling, move your newts to a warmer area to induce breeding. Females produce between 100 and 175 eggs, which they wrap individually in the leaves of aquatic plants. Move the egg-covered vegetation to a separate aquarium, because alpine newts are notorious for eating their own eggs. Larvae can be fed an assortment of live invertebrates, including daphnia, chopped blackworms, and fleshly hatched brine shrimp. At warmer temperatures, larvae complete metamorphosis in less than half a year.

Eastern Newt

The eastern newt (*Notophthalmus viridescens*) ranges throughout the eastern United States and into Canada, where populations inhabit swamps, ponds, and slow-moving streams. Between their aquatic larval and adult life stages they live terrestrially, foraging in leaf litter on the forest floor as they mature. During this stage they are commonly called red efts. While adult eastern newts are predominantly olive-brown with varying amounts of black and red spotting, the juvenile

Eastern newts, especially those from northern populations, are highly cold-tolerant and are sometimes seen moving about in iced-over ponds.

Red Efts

Red efts are the terrestrial form of the eastern newt. They undergo this juvenile stage after completing metamorphosis but before reaching sexual maturity. Red efts can take seven years to mature into mainly aquatic adults, but more often they spend only a few years on land before returning to water. Certain populations are known to transform directly from larvae to adults, skipping the eft stage.

red efts are a brilliant orange-red with two rows of vermilion dots lining their dorsums. This bright coloration helps warn predators of their poisonous nature. The toxicity of efts is ten times more than that of adult newts. Eastern newts stay small, ranging in size from 2.6 inches (6.6 cm) to 5.5 inches (14 cm) in total length. In the wild, aquatic adults feed on most any small animal they can catch, including zooplankton, insect larvae, snails, small fish, and even the eggs of other amphibians. Terrestrial efts eat an assortment of invertebrates, including mites, fly larvae, and small spiders.

Care

In captivity, eastern newts make hardy captives provided you start with individuals in good health. At pet stores they are often housed with other species or in heated aquaria, both of which contribute to the poor condition they are sometimes sold in. When selecting an eastern newt, avoid lethargic individuals, particularly those spending large amounts of time on land.

The housing of adult eastern newts should reflect their mostly aquatic lifestyle, with an environment similar to that described for the Chinese fire-bellied newt (*Cynops orientalis*) working well. Red efts, on the other hand, need a terrestrial setup, with a soil or mulch substrate and a few pieces of driftwood and moss for shelter. A 15-gallon (56.8-l) aquarium is large enough for four adult newts, while a single eft may be housed in a 5-gallon (19-l) aquarium. Eastern newts are tolerant of a range of temperatures. They can permanently be maintained between 60°F (15.6°C) and 70°F (21.1°C), although it may be advantageous to

Because red efts are toxic to predators, they are very bold little creatures that wander far from cover.

expose them to a cool winter period during which temperatures rarely rise above 50°F (10°C) for a couple months.

The diet of adult eastern newts can be composed largely of chopped earthworms, blackworms, and bloodworms. Some individuals also accept prepared pellet diets. Red efts should be fed small crickets, chopped worms, fly larvae, and flightless fruit flies.

Breeding

Breeding in captivity sometimes occurs if strong seasonal changes in temperature are provided, but this is surprisingly uncommon considering the popularity of eastern newts. Males in breeding condition develop nuptial pads on their back legs. Their cloacas also swell during the breeding season. Females produce between 200 and 375 eggs, which they attach singly to aquatic vegetation. Larvae hatch three to five weeks later and take anywhere from two to five months to complete metamorphosis. You will need to decrease water depth and provide access to land as larvae transform into terrestrial efts. Larvae can be fed a diet similar to that provided for aquatic adults but, because of their smaller size, blackworms and earthworms should be cut into pieces. Daphnia and freshly hatched brine shrimp are good for young larvae. Eastern newt larvae are cannibalistic, so take care to sort them by size, keeping smaller individuals together so that they don't become food for their larger siblings.

The Name Game

Recent molecular work has shown that the four previously recognized subspecies of *N. viridescens* are invalid. They are still commonly used in literature, however. The former subspecies include the red-spotted newt (*N. v. viridescens*), central newt (*N. v. louisianensis*), broken-striped newt (*N. v. dorsalis*), and peninsula newt (*N. v. piaropicola*).

Pachytriton labiatus is the most common paddle-tailed newt in captivity, but it is rarely captive bred.

Pachytrition brevipes showing off the enlarged tail that gives the genus the common name paddle-tailed newt.

Paddle-Tailed Newts

The most regularly seen of the species in the genus *Pachytriton*, known as a group by the name paddle-tailed newts, is *Pachytriton labiatus*, which inhabits hilly streams in southeast China. They are sporadically found for sale in pet stores, sometimes being called giant fire-bellied newts. While at first glance paddle-tailed newts can appear like a large version of the Chinese fire-bellied newt, they differ in many ways. Most obvious is their big, laterally compressed tail, which helps them navigate the moving waters they live in and has given rise to their common name. Their heads also clearly differ from those of *Cynops* species, having lips (called labial folds) that slightly overhang the lower jaw. Two orange dotted lines run down the back of some individuals, while the dorsum of others is solid brown. The ventral side of paddle-tailed newts is variable; it can be brick orange dappled in black, or almost solely one of those two colors. As adults, paddle-tailed newts range in size from 5.0 inches (12.7 cm) to 7.0 inches (17.8 cm) in total length.

The Other Paddle-Tails

Another paddle-tailed newt, P. *breviceps*, is infrequently available. It differs in coloration from P. *labiatus*, dorsally being a variable brown with black spots. Three other newts have also been described as *Pachytriton* species, one of which has attractive blue spots on its tail. Their taxonomic status is currently unclear, and they have been described only from individuals in the pet trade.

Heat-Stressed *Pachytriton*

Healthy paddle-tailed newts are fully aquatic. Stressed individuals kept at warm temperatures regularly leave the water. When selecting one, take this into consideration. If your newt spends a lot of time out of the water, check the temperature and cool the enclosure if necessary.

Warty Newts

Occasionally offered for sale in pet stores alongside Chinese fire-bellied newts and paddle-tailed newts are warty newts of the genus *Paramesotriton*. They are sometimes sold as "giant fire-bellied newts." While closely related to *Cynops*, the seven species of warty newts require slightly different care in captivity. They are aggressive, and if kept in groups they must be housed in large enclosures.

Offer a semi-aquatic environment, with a slight current through the water provided by a submersible power filter. Temperatures can vary between 55°F (12.8°C) and 74°F (23.3°C) depending on the time of year. Warty newts feed on an assortment of invertebrates, including chopped worms, blackworms, fly larvae, small crickets, and bloodworms. Breeding in captivity is not well documented but seems to be triggered by seasonal variations in temperature. Females deposit eggs on aquatic vegetation or in dark crevices under rocks during warmer times of the year. After completing metamorphosis, young warty newts often prefer to live terrestrially, and they require a semi-aquatic setup with a large land area.

Care

Although paddle-tailed newts are moderately sized, they require large enclosures because of their aggressive behavior. Males in particular often engage in combat if they are housed together without adequate space. You can keep a male/female pair in a standard 20-gallon (75.7-l) aquarium, though providing more room is recommended. Both simple and natural aquarium designs work well for these aquatic amphibians. If you use a substrate, take care that it either is too large for your paddle-tail to swallow or is fine sand, which will pass easily if ingested. Furnish the aquarium with multiple dark caves and crevices constructed out of rocks, flower pots, PVC plastic pipe segments, or other suitable material. It's a good idea to assemble a secure stack of rocks that break the water's surface in part of the tank. Although paddle-tailed newts are typically aquatic, occasional individuals leave the water during warm conditions. Filtration should consist of a submersible or hang-on-the-tank power filter that oxygenates the water well and creates a moderate current.

Temperature is a crucial component of paddle-tailed newt care. They are hardy animals that tolerate occasional warm days [~70°F (21.1°C)], but their regular temperature level needs to be cool. Maintain your paddle-tails between 50°F (10°C) and 65°F (18.3°C) most of the time. You can accomplish this by keeping their enclosure in a cool area of your house, such as in the basement or on the floor of a cool room.

Paddle-tailed newts eat many different foods, including chopped worms, feeder guppies, bloodworms, and commercially prepared diets. They inhale their food with the suction created as their mouths open underwater. Offer food two to three times a week, less often as their metabolism slows when kept at temperatures on the cool side of the abovementioned range.

Breeding

Paddle-tailed newts are rarely bred in captivity and offer a challenge for experienced amphibian hobbyists. Males are most easily distinguished from females by their enlarged cloacas. They can also be told apart from females by the presence of one or more white spots on the last third of their tails, though these spots become distinct only when males are in breeding condition. Seasonal variations in tem-

Adult (top) and larval (bottom) Spanish ribbed newts. Their sharp rib tips help deter predators.

perature may help stimulate breeding behavior. During a winter cooling, it may be beneficial to house males separately from females. As the temperature warms up, the newts can be reintroduced to each other, which may help encourage courtship. Eggs are laid on the undersides of stones or in aquatic caves. Females guard their eggs fiercely until they hatch, fending off potential predators. The larvae complete metamorphosis quickly and spend their early life on land.

Spanish Ribbed Newt

Capable of growing to 12 inches (30.5 cm) in length, Spanish ribbed newts (*Pleurodeles waltl*) make impressive captives. They are predominantly olive-brown, with blurred charcoal blotches coating their body. Ventrally the brownish color fades to light gray. Down their sides run two raised lightly-colored dotted rows. Under these rows are the sharp tips of their ribs, which they can force through their skin to harm predators when threatened. Found in southern Spain, Portugal, and northern Morocco, Spanish ribbed newts are highly aquatic, inhabiting ponds, ditches, and slow-moving streams. If their body of water dries, they squeeze under rocks and mud to stay moist.

Defensive Ribs

Lining the back of Spanish ribbed newts are two rows of lightly colored warts. Beneath these is an interesting defense mechanism: their ribs. When a Spanish ribbed newt is attacked, their sharp rib tips penetrate their skin as glands secrete a toxin, allowing them to fend off hungry predators. Crocodile newts (*Tylototriton* spp.) are known to have a similar defense mechanism.

Care

Although wild Spanish ribbed newts have been recorded growing to remarkably large sizes, captive individuals generally stay smaller and do not need a large enclosure. A standard 15-gallon (56.8-l) aquarium is enough room for a pair. This should be set up aquatically, ideally being planted with live plants. You can provide a small piece of floating corkbark to allow access out of water, though it will rarely be used. For filtration, you can use a sponge or power filter. Maintain a water temperature between 60°F (15.6°C) and 72°F (22.2°C). Temperatures around 50°F (10°C) are not a problem, but when kept for extended periods of time at temperatures above their preferred range, the newts may suffer from heat stress.

Spanish ribbed newts greedily consume almost any appropriate food. Their diet can include chopped worms, thawed frozen fish foods, and blackworms, but other foods like fly larvae, wax worms, feeder guppies, and pellet diets provide variety.

Breeding

Male Spanish ribbed newts in breeding condition develop nuptial pads on their front legs, which they use to grasp females with during courtship. Males can also be distinguished from females by the sometimes reddish shade of their brown body color. Spanish ribbed newts are easily bred in captivity, often doing so without additional stimulation other than the naturally fluctuating temperatures of an average household. To purposely initiate breeding, consider increasing the temperature, photoperiod, and water depth. Females deposit between 200 and 300 eggs individually or in small clusters in aquatic vegetation or on submerged rocks. The larvae are simple to care for and grow well when kept warm, near 70°F (21.1°C). Feed a diet of daphnia, chopped blackworms, tubifex worms, live brine shrimp, and

Rough-skinned newts range along the west coast from California to Alaska.

California Newt

Similar in appearance to the rough-skinned newt is another *Taricha* species, *T. torosa*. Commonly called the California newt, you can tell this species apart from rough-skinned newts by examining their eyes, which are larger. The lower eyelid is also lightly colored. California newts are more terrestrial than rough-skinned newts, spending much of their time on land near water. In captivity, house them in a semi-aquatic setup with a large land area.

other small invertebrates. Juveniles are highly aquatic like adults and require the same care.

Rough-Skinned Newt

The common name rough-skinned newt is fitting for *Taricha granulosa*, with the seasonally terrestrial adults developing bumpy and irregular skin while living on land. Their backs are chocolate brown, which contrasts with their tangerine-colored bellies. Rough-skinned newts display their bright ventral side to warn potential predators of their toxic nature. They are capable of growing to 8.5 inches (21.6 cm), though some mature at only 5 inches (12.7 cm) in total length. Also regularly called the Oregon newt by the pet trade, *T. granulosa* ranges throughout the Pacific Coast of North America, from California to Alaska. Several weeks after larvae complete metamorphosis, they leave the water to live a secretive existence, hiding on land until they mature. This can take more than five years. Adults are semi-aquatic and, depending on the population, return to the water for a few months of the year to breed or spend most of their adult lives aquatically.

Tetradotoxin

A powerful neurotoxin called tetradotoxin is found in the skin of some amphibians, including the commonly available rough-skinned newt and eastern newt. Provided you don't eat your newts, you have little to worry about, but because of the danger it's best to avoid interaction with them.

Care

Rough-skinned newts do well in captivity. A standard 20-gallon (75.7-l) aquarium is enough room for a trio of adult newts. The water depth should exceed 10 inches (25.4 cm) in part of the aquarium, with shallow areas being available elsewhere. A well-planted semi-aquatic setup with interesting driftwood and rocks jutting out of the water creates an attractive display well-suited to rough-skinned newts. Alternatively, you can use a bare-bottom setup, with their land area being created with a platform, like a floating piece of corkbark. Certain individual rough-skinned newts are more terrestrial than others, so pay attention to your particular newts and increase or decrease the size of the land area as appropriate.

Ideally, the temperature in the tank should stay between 50°F (10°C) and 70°F (21.1°C). Rough-skinned newts tolerate warmer temperatures poorly, but days or even weeks of temperatures below 50°F (10°C) are fine.

Feed rough-skinned newts a varied diet consisting of blackworms, leaf worms, chopped nightcrawlers, small crickets, and fly larvae. Many also accept thawed frozen fish foods such as bloodworms and tubifex worms.

Breeding

On average, male rough-skinned newts are slightly larger than females. They develop a swollen cloaca, nuptial pads on their back legs and toes, and a slight tail fin when in breeding condition. Breeding in the wild occurs throughout the year, but typically it starts after a cool winter. You can coax your captive rough-skinned newts to breed by exposing them to seasonal variations in temperature. During the

The dorsal crest on this male northern crested newt is not well developed, indicating he is just entering or just past breeding condition.

winter, the newts can be moved to a cool basement or garage. Ensure that the temperature does not fall below 40°F (4.4°C) for extended periods of time. Alternatively, you can experiment by placing rough-skinned newts into the refrigerator to cool them if the temperature in your area does not decrease significantly in the winter. Your newts will likely spend most of their time on land during a cool winter period. An increase in temperature following winter months should trigger breeding behavior. In the wild, hundreds and even thousands of rough-skinned newts breed at one time. They lay their eggs singly on aquatic vegetation, usually close to the water's surface. Larvae take anywhere from four months to nearly one year to complete metamorphosis in the wild. With the pet trade relying almost solely on wild-caught rough-skinned newts for stock, it's well worth your time to breed them in captivity.

Northern Crested Newt

One of Europe's most common newts is the northern crested newt (Triturus cristatus). They inhabit forest ponds, flooded ditches, gardens, irrigation channels, and other areas with small, slow-moving to stagnant bodies of water. During the breeding season, males develop an enlarged jagged dorsal crest, which they display to females during courtship. With their gaudy toothed crest spanning the length of the dorsum and tail, males look like miniature aquatic dragons when in breeding condition. Crested newts are dark on top, with white flecks bordering their orange and black-spotted bellies. Females are capable of growing to 7.2 inches (18.3 cm) in total length, while the smaller males reach 6.4 inches (16.3 cm).

They are seasonally aquatic, leaving the water as temperatures cool in the fall to enter a state of torpor on land. As temperatures warm in the spring, the newts return to water to live aquatically and breed.

The Other Crested Newts

The Italian crested newt (T. *carnifex*), the Danube crested newt (T. *dobrogicus*), and the southern crested newt (T. *karelinii*) are occasionally available, and their care is identical to that of the northern crested newt. Although their care is the same, avoid housing the different species together to prevent interbreeding.

Crested Cannibalism

Crested newt larvae are notorious cannibals. Sort them by size to prevent larger individuals from eating smaller ones.

Care

Hardy and easily bred, northern crested newts are a good choice as a first newt to keep. They are best located through newt breeders. A trio will live happily in a standard 15-gallon (56.8-l) aquarium. Offer aquatic vegetation for resting spots near the water's surface, as well as a land area that takes up around one-quarter of the floor space. At warmer temperatures, it's rare for crested newts to leave water. Water depth can be as shallow as 5 inches (12.7 cm), though deeper water does not present a problem. You can use a sponge filter for filtration, though in a large aquarium that is lightly stocked, a filter may not be necessary. Maintain a temperature between 55°F (12.8°C) and 70°F (21.1°C) most of the year. Healthy crested newts will tolerate occasional days outside of this range.

Food can consist of worms, blackworms, wax worms, bloodworms, tubifex worms, and large daphnia. For newts that move onto land during cool conditions, offer small crickets.

Male marbled newt with a fully developed crest. This is a terrestrial species that becomes aquatic during the breeding season.

Triturus Hybrids

The marbled newt and crested newt interbreed in certain ponds where their ranges overlap. At one time the hybrids were classified as a separate species, *Triturus blasii*.

Breeding

Males crested newts are easy to distinguish from females by their enlarged cloacas, which are black in color. In contrast, the female's cloaca is reduced in size and yellowish, a color that also extends down her tail. During the breeding season, the difference between sexes becomes more pronounced, as the males develop an enlarged dorsal crest and silver tail stripes. Breeding occurs in the wild following a cool winter, and if you want to breed your newts you should provide seasonal variations. By keeping their enclosure in a cool garage or basement during the winter, a temperature decrease can be provided, during which the newts will likely move to land. Sometimes the seasonal variations in temperature in a room are enough to trigger a breeding response. Temperatures as low as 40°F (4.4°C) do not present a problem, but at these cold temperatures the newt's metabolism slows considerably and they require little food.

As temperatures warm in spring, crested newts return to water. Males develop their impressive crest at this point and begin courting females. Females fold their eggs individually within the leaves of aquatic vegetation. Many people provide anacharis (*Elodea densa*) as egg-deposition sites. You can also give the newts strips of thin plastic for egg deposition. Remove the eggs as soon as you notice them to prevent the adults from eating them. Over the course of the breeding season, a captive female can lay nearly 1500 eggs, though she is more likely to produce between 300 and 500. Care for the larvae is fairly typical. When kept at a temperature near 65°F (18°C), they complete metamorphosis in three to four months. In the wild, juveniles live terrestrially, but in captivity they can be kept aquatically to make feeding easier. Crested newts reach maturity as early as one year following metamorphosis.

Marbled Newt

With rough emerald green skin patterned in black blotches and an orange dorsal stripe, the marbled newt (*Triturus marmoratus*) is an attractive captive. Individuals are moderately sized, with the largest growing to slightly over 6 inches (15.2 cm). Males are often smaller than females and as adults lack an orange dorsal stripe. Marbled newts range throughout much of France, northern Spain, and Portugal. They are seasonally aquatic, living on land until the breeding season, during which they enter temporary or permanent ponds for part of the year to spawn.

Care

Marbled newts are easily cared for. They are bred frequently in captivity and are best acquired directly from breeders. There are several approaches to housing marbled newts. Throughout cooler periods of the year you can house marbled newts in a terrestrial setup that incorporates a soil substrate, small water dish, and several hide spots. As temperatures warm,

Mandarin newts are commonly available in the hobby in the United States, but they are rarely captive bred.

place mature individuals into a heavily planted aquarium for breeding. Perhaps a better way to keep them is in a large aquarium designed to house them year-round. You can partition the tank into equal parts land and water, securely stacking rocks to form easy access to the land section. Maintain a temperature between 55°F (12.8°C) and 72°F (22.2°C), and feed a diet of live worms, crickets, wax worms, fly larvae, blackworms, and thawed frozen foods.

Breeding

If breeding is your goal, you will need to expose the newts to seasonal changes. During the winter, the temperature should stay below 50°F (10°C). Your newts will live terrestrially at these cold temperatures, and because their metabolism slows, they only need to be fed occasionally. If a cool basement or garage is unavailable, consider refrigerating your newts. Following the cool winter, you can gradually increase the temperature. If all has gone as planned, the newts will enter water once warmed up. The male's dorsal ridge dramatically increases in size at this time. Females lay up to 400 eggs, though quantities less than half this size are more common. It takes larvae two to four months to reach nearly 3.0 inches (7.6 cm) in length, at which point they complete metamorphosis and leave the water. Keep juveniles in a small terrestrial setup, with a shallow water dish. Feed flightless fruit flies, crickets, and small worms coated in appropriate vitamin and mineral supplements to them daily.

The Mandarin Newt

Tylototriton shanjing, commonly called the mandarin or emperor newt, appears very similar to the crocodile newt. *T. shanjing* differs from *T. verrucosus* by its terrestrial lifestyle and the greater degree of orange patterning on the body. In contrast to the crocodile newt, mandarin newts prefer a terrestrial setup, with only a small, shallow water dish. Maintain them at a temperature similar that used for crocodile newts, offering a diet of crickets, worms, and grubs. Pet stores and dealers may confuse the mandarin newt with the crocodile newt because of their similar appearance, so take care to identify which species you acquire so you can care for them properly.

Crocodile Newt

The crocodile newt (*Tylototriton verrucosus*) can be found for sale under a variety of names, including crocodile newt, emperor newt, knobby newt, and Himalayan crocodile newt. Down their dorsal side run two sets of raised orange bumps, in between which is a solid stripe. Their heads appear crowned in this same orange color, with a large bumpy crest wrapping around it. There are several different forms of crocodile newt, with somewhat different body structures and coloration. Individuals from certain populations are less colorful than others. As adults, crocodile newts have been recorded reaching 9 inches (23 cm) in total length, though most attain barely a length near 7 inches (17.8 cm). They are native to southeast Asia, where they inhabit moist forest streams and permanent ponds.

Care

Crocodile newts are impressive animals to keep because of their exotic appearance. Unfortunately, they are only occasionally bred in captivity, and wild-caught animals dominate the pet trade. Do your best searching for a breeder, because newts born in captivity typically fare better than those from the wild. A trio of adult crocodile newts can be kept in a standard 20-gallon (75.7-l) aquarium, set up aquatically with a section of floating cork-bark, driftwood, or other object protruding from the water's surface. At cool temperatures, crocodile newts may leave the water, but when kept at average household temperatures they remain aquatic. Avoid temperatures above 77°F (25°C), maintaining the water between 60°F (15.6°C) and 70°F (21.1°C) most of the time.

Crocodile newts are avid, even greedy, feeders. Offer a diet of leaf worms, chopped night crawlers, bloodworms, tubifex worms, waxworms, and other soft-bodied invertebrates, feeding every few days.

Breeding

Breeding occasionally occurs in captivity but not as often as you would like for such an attractively patterned and bold newt. The few published accounts of captive breeding report that changes in temperature initiate breeding behavior, with increases of just 10°F (6°C) being adequate stimuli. In the wild, they are seasonal breeders, with some populations over-wintering on land and returning to water as the weather warms. If exposing crocodile newts to cool temperatures below 60°F (15.6°C) for breeding purposes, provide a large land area for them to retreat to.

Amphiumas

Amphiumas (family Amphiumidae) are native to the southeastern United States, where they live aquatically in ponds, ditches, swamps, and occasionally slow-moving streams. They have elongated eel-like bodies with only tiny, nearly useless, limbs. Also commonly called Congo eels, amphiumas spend much of the day hiding in crayfish burrows. At night they emerge to hunt crustaceans, worms, and other aquatic creatures. Sometimes amphiumas are found on land while moving to a new water source during a heavy rain. They can remain submerged in their muddy burrows during dry conditions, going without food for months.

The family Amphiumidae contains one genus (*Amphiuma*) with three species. The largest is the two-toed amphiuma (*Amphiuma means*), capable of growing to nearly four feet (1.2 m) in length. The three-toed amphiuma (*Amphiuma tridactylum*) can mature at near a similar monstrous size. The smallest member of Amphiumidae is the one-toed amphi-

The dark form of the crocodile newt in a planted aquarium.

uma (*Amphiuma pholeter*), with the largest individuals growing slightly over 1 foot (0.3 m) in total length. As their common names suggest, the somewhat similar two-toed and three-toed amphiumas can be told apart by counting their toes. The one-toed amphiuma has only one toe and does not grow nearly as large as the others.

Care

Two-toed and three-toed amphiumas are periodically available from herp dealers and sellers on the Internet. As voracious predators, they make impressive captives, attacking most anything they sense moving near them. Provide your amphiuma with an aquarium in excess of 30-gallons (113.5-l). Amphiumas are good at escaping, so make sure the cover used fits securely around the top, and consider filling tall tanks only halfway with water to further discourage escapes. A bare-bottom setup can be used to facilitate partial water changes, which should be performed weekly. Use an external power filter or sponge filter to help maintain water quality. Growing a layer of floating vegetation on the water's surface will help keep nitrates in check and nuisance algae to a minimum. You can furnish the aquarium with PVC plastic pipe segments, driftwood, and aquarium decorations that offer dark hiding spots. These are important so that your amphiuma feels secure. Always keep the water temperature below 80°F (26.7°C).

Feeding amphiumas is a thrill. As food enters the aquarium, they slowly sniff around to locate it. Once they have crept close, they ambush the prey at lightning speed, clamping down hard with their power-ful jaws. (Amphiumas are reported to have a particu-larly painful bite, so use cau-tion when transporting or feeding them.) Offer a diet consisting largely of night-crawlers, crayfish, cooked or raw cocktail shrimp (avoid those with added salts or fla-voring), and whole fish. Many also become accus-tomed to eating large-pellet fish foods. Amphiumas will consume almost any animal they can capture, so be wary of housing them with others.

The one-toed amphiuma is found in Florida, southern Alabama, and southern Georgia.

Sirens

From afar, sirens (family Sirenidae) may appear similar to amphiumas, but when examined closely they differ in many ways. Most notably, sirens lack hind limbs. They also retain their larval gills as adults, which appear as bushy red frills at the back of their heads.

There are four species of sirens: the southern dwarf siren (*Pseudobranchus axanthus*), the northern dwarf siren (*P. striatus*), the lesser siren (*Siren intermedia*) and the greater siren (*S. lacertina*). The two dwarf sirens grow to under a foot in length, sometimes maturing at less than 5 inches (12.7 cm). The other two *Siren* species grow larger, with the greater siren recorded at a maximum of 38.6 inches (98 cm) in total length. In captivity, house sirens in an aquatic setup with little current. Maintain the water

The greater siren ranges from Maryland to Alabama.

temperature between 65°F (18.3°C) and 80°F (26.7°C), avoiding warmer conditions. Feed dwarf sirens a diet of small invertebrates, such as blackworms, bloodworms, and tubifex worms. Lesser and greater sirens require larger food, like leaf worms, nightcrawlers, and occasional small fish.

Breeding

Amphiumas have yet to be bred in captivity. This provides you with a great opportunity to document something nobody before you has. Seasonal changes in water level, temperature, and photoperiod may possibly encourage breeding behavior. In the wild, females lay around 200 eggs in nesting cavities, with larval amphiumas hatching at around 2.5 inches (6.4 cm) in length. Larval amphiumas have been observed schooling in the wild.

References

AmphibiaWeb. 2006. University of Berkeley California. Accessed winter 2008. http://amphibiaweb.org/index.html.

Azizi, Emanuel, and Tobias Landberg. Effects of metamorphosis on the aquatic escape response of the two-lined salamander (*Eurycea Bislineata*). *The Journal of Experimental Biology*. 205 (2002): 841-849.

Bakkers, Mark, and Wouter Beukema. Tylototriton.org. 2007. Accessed spring 2008. http://www.tylototriton.org.

Bartlett, R. D. Attractive, Hardy, and Just a Little Bit Toxic: the Flashy Firebellies. *Tropical Fish Hobbyist*. July 1995.

Bartlett, Dick. Waterdogs and Axolotls. *Reptiles*. Feb. 2002.

Bernard, Joni, Mary Allen, and Duane Ullrey. Feeding captive insectivorous animals: nutritional aspects of insects as food. *Nutrition Advisory Group Handbook*. (1997).

Bernardo, Joseph, and Stevan J. Arnold. Mass-rearing of Plethodontid salamander eggs. *Amphibia-Reptilia*. 20 (1999): 219-224.

COSEWIC. Assessment and update status report on the Allegheny Mountain Dusky Salamander *Desmognathus ochrophaeus* (Great Lakes/St. Lawrence population and Carolinian population) in Canada. Committee on the Status of Endangered Wildlife in Canada. Ottawa. 2007.

Dresens, Harry. Harry's Salamanderweb. Accessed winter 2008. http://www.salamanders.nl.nu/.

Gabor, Caitlin R., and Chris C. Nice. Genetic variation among populations of Eastern Newts, *Notophthalmus viridescens*: a preliminary analysis based on allozymes. *Herpetologica*. 60 (2004): 373-386.

Griffiths, Richard A. *Newts and Salamanders of Europe*. London and San Diego: Academic P, 1996.

Hofrichter, Robert, ed. *The Encyclodpedia of Amphibians*. Toronto: Key Porter Books, 2000.

Indiviglio, Frank. *Newts and Salamanders*. Hauppauge, NY: Barron's, 1997.

IUCN, Conservation International, and NatureServe. 2006. Global Amphibian Assessment. Accessed winter 2008. www.globalamphibians.org.

Klaus-Detlef, Kühnel. Raising *Triturus cristatus*. *Tropical Fish Hobbyist*. Nov. 1991: 128-136.

Kowalski, Edward. Captive Care and Maintenance of Slimy Salamanders. *Reptiles*. June 2002: 48-57.

Kowalski, Edward. Keep Your Marbles. *Reptiles*. June 2001.

Kozak, Kenneth H. Sexual isolation and courtship behavior in salamanders of the *Eurycea bislineata* species complex, with comments on the evolution of the mental gland and pheromone delivery behavior in the Plethodontidae. *Southeastern Naturalist*. 2 (2003): 281-292.

Lembcke, Peter. Personal interview. 14 Jan. 2008.

Macke, Jennifer, comp. Caudata Culture. Accessed winter 2008. http://www.caudata.org/cc/.

Mattison, Chris. *Keeping and Breeding Amphibians*. London: Blandford, 1993.

Miller, Jessica J. Caudata. Living Underworld. Accessed winter 2008. http://www.livingunderworld.org/caudata/.

National Audubon Society. *Field Guide to Reptiles and Amphibians of North America*. New York: Alfred a. Knopf Inc., 1979.

Nigrelli, R.F. Some longevity records of vertebrates. *Transactions of the New York Academy of Science*. 16 (1954):296-299.

Nowak, Robert T., and Edmund D. Brodie Jr. Rib penetration and associated antipredator adaptations in the salamander *Pleurodeles waltl* (Salamandridae). *Copeia*. 1978 (1978): 424-429.

Petranka, James W. *Salamanders of the United States and Canada*. Washington and London: Smithsonian Institution P, 1998.

Quinn, Vanessa S., and Brent M. Graves. A technique for sexing red-backed salamanders. *Herpetological Review*. 30 (1999).

Rogner, Manfred. The Fire Salamander. *Tropical Fish Hobbyist*. Sep.1996: 134-142.

Savage, Jay M. *The Amphibians and Reptiles of Costa Rica*. Chicago, IL: University of Chicago P, 2002.

Sparreboom, Max, and Burkhard Thiesmeier. Courtship behavior of *Pachytriton labiatus*. *Amphibia-Reptilia*. 20 (1999): 339-344.

Staniszewski, Marc. Alpine Newt (*Triturus Alpestris*) Care Sheet. Accessed winter 2008. http://www.amphibian.co.uk/alpine.html.

Staniszewski, Marc. *Amphibians in Captivity*. Neptune City, NJ: T.F.H., 1995.

Steinfartz, Sebastian, Michael Veith, and Diethard Tautz. Mitochondrial sequence analysis of *Salamandra* taxa suggests old splits of major lineages and postglacial recolonizations of central Europe from distinct source populations of *Salamandra salamandra*." *Molecular Ecology*. 9 (2000): 397-410.

Thiesmeier, Burkhard. Notes on the Salamandrid genus *Pachytriton*. *Herpetologia Bonnensis* (1997): 353-358.

Wisniewski, Pat. The Fire Salamander in Legend and in Captivity. *Aquarist and Pondkeeper*. Dec. 1986: 39-41.

Wisniewski, P.J., and L.M. Paull. Breeding and Rearing the European Fire Salamander. *International Zoo Yearbook*. 24/25 (1986): 223-226.

Wisniewski, P. Captive Husbandry of the Fire Salamander. *ASRA Monographs*. 2 (1987).

Resources

Clubs & Societies

Amphibian, Reptile & Insect Association
Liz Price
23 Windmill Rd
Irthlingsborough
Wellingborough NN9 5RJ
England

American Society of Ichthyologists and Herpetologists
Maureen Donnelly, Secretary
Grice Marine Laboratory
Florida International University
Biological Sciences
11200 SW 8th St.
Miami, FL 33199
Telephone: (305) 348-1235
E-mail: asih@fiu.edu
www.asih.org

Society for the Study of Amphibians and Reptiles (SSAR)
Marion Preest, Secretary
The Claremont Colleges
925 N. Mills Ave.
Claremont, CA 91711
Telephone: 909-607-8014
E-mail:
mpreest@jsd.claremont.edu
www.ssarherps.org

Web Sites

Amphibiancare.com (author's website)
www.amphibiancare.com/frogs/main.html

Amphibian Specialist Group
www.amphibians.org.

Axolotls
www.axolotl.org/

Caudata.org Newt and Salamander Portal
www.caudata.org/

Caudata Culture
www.caudata.org/cc/

Livingunderworld.org: A Web Project About Amphibians
www.livingunderworld.org/

Marc Staniszewski's Amphibian Information Centre
www.amphibian.co.uk/

Melissa Kaplan's Herp Care Collection
http://www.anapsid.org/

The Reptile Rooms
www.reptilerooms.org/

Robyn's Salamander and Newt Page
www.fishpondinfo.com/saly.htm

Super Newt
http://newt150.tripod.com/

Index

3 1143 00900 3451